W9-BSR-552

STERLING BIOGRAPHIES

ELEANOR ROOSEVELT

A Courageous Spirit

Victoria Garrett Jones

Sterling Publishing Co., Inc.
New York

I am very grateful to Heather Quinlan at Sterling Publishing for giving me the opportunity to produce this work. Her insightful comments and thoughtful guidance have been invaluable. I would also like to thank my husband, George, and my friends, Missy, Millie, Lynna, and Kathi, for their encouragement over the past year.

To Doreen Neugebauer Sanzone, whose unconditional support and unwavering friendship have enriched my life for three decades, I dedicate this volume.

Library of Congress Cataloging-in-Publication Data

Jones, Victoria Garrett.
  Eleanor Roosevelt : a courageous spirit / Victoria Garrett Jones.
      p. cm. -- (Sterling biographies)
  Includes bibliographical references and index.
  ISBN-13: 978-1-4027-3371-0
  ISBN-10: 1-4027-3371-2
1. Roosevelt, Eleanor, 1884-1962--Juvenile literature. 2.   Presidents' spouses--United States--
Biography--Juvenile literature. 1. Title.

E807.1.R48J66 2007
973.917092--dc22
[B]

                                                                    2006027149

---

10 9 8 7 6 5 4 3 2 1

Published by Sterling Publishing Co., Inc.
387 Park Avenue South, New York, NY 10016

© 2007 by Victoria Garrett Jones

Distributed in Canada by Sterling Publishing
C/o Canadian Manda Group, 165 Dufferin Street
Toronto, Ontario, Canada M6K 3H6

Distributed in the United Kingdom by GMC Distribution Services
Castle Place, 166 High Street, Lewes, East Sussex, England BN7 1XU
Distributed in Australia by Capricorn Link (Australia) Pty. Ltd.
P.O. Box 704, Windsor, NSW 2756, Australia

Printed in China
All rights reserved

Sterling ISBN-13: 978-1-4027-3371-0 (paperback)
      ISBN-10: 1-4027-3371-2

Sterling ISBN-13: 978-1-4027-4746-5 (hardcover)
      ISBN-10: 1-4027-4746-2

Designed by Patrice Sheridan
Image research by Susan Schader

For information about custom editions, special sales, premium and
corporate purchases, please contact Sterling Special Sales
Department at 800-805-5489 or specialsales@sterlingpub.com.

Contents

INTRODUCTION: A Courageous Spirit 1

CHAPTER 1: The Roosevelts 4

CHAPTER 2: Childhood of Sorrow 12

CHAPTER 3: For Better or Worse 20

CHAPTER 4: Years of Change .34

CHAPTER 5: Beating the Odds .46

CHAPTER 6: The Road to Higher Office 59

CHAPTER 7: The President's Wife 73

CHAPTER 8: Taking a Stand 86

CHAPTER 9: The Last Term 97

CHAPTER 10: First Lady of the World 110

GLOSSARY 120

BIBLIOGRAPHY 121

IMAGE CREDITS 122

ABOUT THE AUTHOR 122

INDEX 123

Events in the Life of Eleanor Roosevelt

1884

October 11, 1884
Born in New York City.

December 1892
Death of Anna Hall Roosevelt, her mother.

August 14, 1894
Death of Elliott Roosevelt, her father.

1899–1902
Student at Allenswood Academy in England, just outside London.

December 11, 1902
Returns to New York and makes her society debut.

1903–04
Volunteer work includes teaching in New York City slums and also investigating immigrant working conditions as member of the National Consumers' League.

March 17, 1905
Marries Franklin D. Roosevelt (FDR).

1918
Volunteers with the American Red Cross in Washington, D.C., during WWI.

1910
FDR is elected to NY State Senate.

1920
Joins the League of Women Voters and eventually becomes chairperson of their Legislative Affairs Committee.

1919
Volunteers at St. Elizabeth's Hospital, visiting sick veterans, and successfully lobbies Congress to improve the facility's conditions.

August 9, 1921
FDR contracts polio and becomes paralyzed.

1922
Joins Women's Trade Union League to promote the women's labor movement, and Women's Division of New York's Democratic State Committee to help organize Democratic women throughout the state.

1928
The Democratic National Committee appoints Eleanor as director of Bureau of Women's Activities. FDR is elected governor of New York in November.

November 8, 1932
FDR elected president.

March 6, 1933
First presidential wife to hold a press conference; only female reporters are invited.

December 30, 1935
Submits her first "My Day" column for publication.

October 24, 1945
The UN is formally established, and President Truman asks Eleanor to become one of its U.S. delegates.

April 12, 1945
FDR dies at his retreat in Warm Springs, Georgia.

1961
Chairs first President's Commission on the Status of Women for the UN.

December 10, 1948
The Universal Declaration of Human Rights, which Eleanor has specifically helped organize, is presented to the UN.

1963
Final book, *Tomorrow Is Now*, is published.

November 7, 1962
Dies in New York City at the age of 78.

1963

A Courageous Spirit

*Courage is more exhilarating than fear
and in the long run it is easier.
We do not have to become heroes overnight.
Just a step at a time, meeting each thing that
comes up, seeing it is not as dreadful as it
appeared, discovering we have the strength
to stare it down.*

Clear, true, and strong, the applause rang out. It filled the flag-draped **United Nations (UN)** hall like the sound of thunder as one by one, country by country, delegates rose in a rare demonstration of personal tribute. Statesmen of all races, creeds, ages, and nationalities temporarily set aside their differences and joined together to honor the accomplishments of a single individual: Eleanor Roosevelt.

It was three a.m. December 10, 1948, and the Universal Declaration of Human Rights had just been passed by the General Assembly of the United Nations. For two years, during the early stages of the **Cold War**—at a time when world tensions were rising to new heights— Eleanor Roosevelt had painstakingly led a **delegation** of eighteen statesmen through eighty-five grueling sessions of deliberations. The result was a document that even today, nearly sixty years later, remains the cornerstone of

During her 12 years in the White House, Eleanor Roosevelt transformed the role of first lady and became a source of inspiration to millions. This portrait was taken four months after her husband's 1933 inauguration.

international human rights. To Eleanor Roosevelt, it would stand as the single greatest achievement of her life.

And what of this life? Who was this tireless worker, this skillful negotiator, and this spokeswoman for the rights of mankind?

Orphaned at ten years old, Eleanor endured a grim childhood. After her marriage in 1905 to Franklin Roosevelt, a distant cousin, she bore six children in ten years. Timid and uncertain, the young Eleanor yielded easily to the wishes of her strong-willed mother-in-law. However, the twin blows of marital betrayal and her husband's paralysis changed the path of Eleanor's future.

Reluctantly stepping in to keep Franklin's political career alive while he battled the aftereffects of polio, Eleanor herself eventually became a force to be reckoned with. As her confidence grew, so did her transformation into an outspoken **activist** for social freedoms. She worked tirelessly for people who were poor or oppressed. Although some critics cruelly made fun of her sensible shoes, simple attire, and lack of glamour, most people looked beneath the surface and were drawn to her sincerity.

With each step in her husband's advancing political career, Eleanor Roosevelt managed to juggle numerous commitments to spouse, society, and self. As first lady, she set a new standard by which all subsequent holders of that position have been judged. Traveling at home and abroad, she logged countless miles on land, at sea, and in the sky, and her face became as familiar to millions as her husband's.

In her widowhood, she easily stepped into the role of diplomat, guiding a multinational UN committee to its finest hour. Eleanor was tireless in her efforts as a **humanitarian**, traveling around the globe and speaking out for the rights of humankind. Modestly downplaying her many accomplishments, she said, "I just did what I had to do as things came along."

In her final book, *Tomorrow Is Now*, Eleanor Roosevelt wrote "One thing I believe profoundly—we make our own history." Perhaps more important, while making her own history, this compassionate and dynamic woman helped to shape the course of humanity. Even today, more than a century after her birth, Eleanor Roosevelt is still considered one of the most admired women the world has ever known.

CHAPTER 1

The Roosevelts

The story of every family is the stuff from which both novels and eventually history is written.

In 1905, Eleanor Roosevelt's marriage to her cousin Franklin brought together two branches of a family that traced their beginnings to one man—Claes Martenszen van Rosenvelt. Van Rosenvelt was born in Holland and in the 1640s settled in the Dutch colony of New Amsterdam—a colony that would one day become New York City.

His son, Nicholas, changed his last name to "Roosevelt" and became the first in the family to hold public office. Throughout the generations, their fortunes grew, and by 1800, there were more than fifty Roosevelt families living in the New York City area.

Theodore Roosevelt Sr. headed up one of these families in the 1800s. His son, Theodore Jr., would one day become president. His other son, Elliott, would one day become father of a first lady, Eleanor.

Born in Holland, Claes Martenszen van Rosenvelt was the first of the Roosevelt family ancestors to settle in North America.

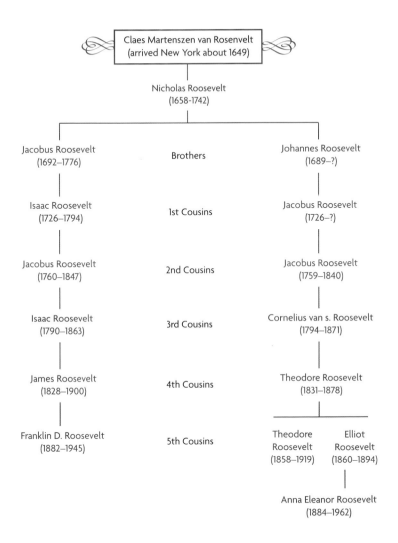

Claes Martenszen van Rosenvelt
(arrived New York about 1649)

Nicholas Roosevelt
(1658-1742)

Jacobus Roosevelt (1692–1776)	Brothers	Johannes Roosevelt (1689–?)
Isaac Roosevelt (1726–1794)	1st Cousins	Jacobus Roosevelt (1726–?)
Jacobus Roosevelt (1760–1847)	2nd Cousins	Jacobus Roosevelt (1759–1840)
Isaac Roosevelt (1790–1863)	3rd Cousins	Cornelius van s. Roosevelt (1794–1871)
James Roosevelt (1828–1900)	4th Cousins	Theodore Roosevelt (1831–1878)
Franklin D. Roosevelt (1882–1945)	5th Cousins	Theodore Roosevelt (1858–1919) / Elliot Roosevelt (1860–1894)

Anna Eleanor Roosevelt
(1884–1962)

Elliott, the family favorite, was prone toward sadness—and dealt with his depression by drinking. In 1883, he met and fell in love with the beautiful Anna Hall. When the young couple became engaged, Elliott's family was sure that married life would

make him happier and lessen his
drinking.

Anna Rebecca Livingston
Ludlow Hall came from a wealthy,
handsome, and distinguished
family. (One of Anna's ancestors had
signed the Declaration of
Independence, and another had given
the oath of office to George Washington
when he became president.) The four Hall
sisters were also known for their beauty.
Clearly, Anna was quite a catch.

Described in the *New York Herald* as "one of
the most brilliant social events of the season," the
wedding of Anna Hall and Elliott Roosevelt took
place in New York City on December 1, 1883. In
the first few months after their marriage,
Elliott did not drink as much, and
the dashing young Roosevelts
were sought after by other
wealthy New Yorkers.

Only two months later, on
Valentine's Day, 1884, tragedy
struck the Roosevelt family when

Wealthy and beautiful, Anna Rebecca Hall
was the oldest of six children. Her 1883
marriage to Elliott Roosevelt
united two socially prominent families.

Elliott's mother, Mittie, died of typhoid fever. Elliott was inconsolable and drank heavily. Anna, already pregnant with their first child, didn't know how to cope with this frightening side of her husband. Although the young couple's future seemed uncertain, friends and family hoped that the joys of parenthood would change their lives for the better again. It was into this troubled family that Anna Eleanor Roosevelt was born on October 11, 1884. Not long after, Eleanor's two brothers arrived—Elliott Jr. in 1889 and Hall in 1891. By her own account and those of others who knew her, Eleanor's childhood was not a happy one. It was dominated by both tragedy and disappointment.

Eleanor was the first of three children born to Anna and Elliott. She later described herself, shown here at age three, as a "shy, solemn child."

Her Father's Daughter

Beautiful, yet self-centered, Anna Hall Roosevelt was affectionate with her sons but cool and distant with her daughter. Eleanor was often left in the company of a nurse or nanny, at least one of whom spoke almost exclusively in French.

In front of family and friends, Anna referred to the shy and solemn child as "Granny." Frequently critical, Anna would tell Eleanor, "You have no looks, so see to it that you have manners."

Eleanor, though rarely at ease in her mother's company, was in awe of Anna's elegance. "She looked so beautiful," Eleanor wrote many years later, "I was grateful to be allowed to touch her dress or her jewels or anything that was part of the vision which I admired."

It was with her father that Eleanor was the happiest. Fun-loving, attractive, and—in his daughter's words—"loved by all who came in contact with him," Elliott Roosevelt appeared devoted to the daughter he called "little Nell." However, although Elliott could be very charming, he was a deeply troubled man. His drinking would eventually ruin any attempts at family happiness. He disappeared for hours—or even days—at a time; Elliott's behavior became increasingly unpredictable.

Once, when walking with young Eleanor and the family's three dogs, Elliott stopped in the Knickerbocker Club for a drink. Hours later, while Eleanor was still patiently waiting on the club's front steps, a drunken Elliott was carried from the building. The club's doorman made sure she got home.

Concerned for the safety of her children and dreading society gossip, Anna begged her husband to change his behavior. During a family holiday to Europe, Elliott checked in and out of several clinics hoping for a "cure." Overwhelmed by responsibilities, Anna sent Eleanor to a convent school

Deeply loved by Eleanor, his only daughter, Elliott Roosevelt struggled with depression for most of his adult life. "He was," Eleanor once wrote, "the center of my world."

outside Paris. Eleanor felt miserable and abandoned by her family. Rather than improving, Elliott's behavior became worse. Believing that the situation was hopeless, Anna eventually returned home with her three

Eleanor, though rarely at ease in her mother's company, was in awe of Anna's elegance.

children, leaving her husband behind in Europe. By now, Elliott's drinking had made the pages of gossip columns. An article in the *New York Herald* proclaimed, "Elliott Roosevelt demented by excesses. Wrecked by liquor and folly, he is now confined in an asylum for the insane near Paris."

His Brother's Keeper

At this point, his brother stepped in. Escorting Elliott home from Europe, Theodore Roosevelt Jr. laid down the law. Elliott must move away from his family—and remain away for at least one year. Elliott must give up drinking and become more responsible. Elliott agreed to these terms and settled in Abingdon, Virginia, where it was arranged that he would help manage the family's mining interests. Now age eight, Eleanor could not understand why her beloved father had been sent away and why she could not go to him. Elliott's letters, which did not come very often, offered little consolation. Yet Eleanor carried the precious letters with her everywhere.

Although Anna tried to focus on raising her children, she was very unhappy. Elliott's behavior, and the gossip resulting from it, embarrassed her deeply. Complaining of painful headaches, Anna spent hours in her darkened bedroom. Shy and timid, Eleanor sometimes sat quietly by her mother's side, gently stroking Anna's forehead. "She was willing to let me sit there for

Elliott (at left, with pipe) poses with his older brother, Theodore, prior to an 1880 hunting trip.

hours on end," Eleanor wrote in her autobiography. "The feeling that I was useful was perhaps the greatest joy I experienced."

Just before Christmas in 1892, Anna Hall Roosevelt died at age twenty-nine from diphtheria. No antibiotics or vaccines were yet available to stop the disease's spread. At the first sign of the illness, Eleanor and her brothers had been sent to the home of a family friend. Elliott, receiving word in Virginia of his wife's illness, hurried to her side—but arrived too late.

When told of her mother's death, Eleanor would later write that "Death meant nothing to me, and one fact wiped out everything else. My father was back and I would see him very soon." But the man who returned to Eleanor from Virginia had changed dramatically. The death of his young wife—with a hoped-for reconciliation no longer a possibility—dealt Elliott a crushing blow from which he would never recover. He sank back into sadness and depression.

Elliott sits with Eleanor and his two sons—Elliott, Jr. at right, and Hall, on his father's lap. Sadly, the younger Elliott would die from diphtheria before his fourth birthday.

CHAPTER 2

Childhood of Sorrow

I was a solemn child, without beauty and painfully shy.

With the death of their mother, and their father's continued failure to change his life, Eleanor, Elliott, and baby Hall were sent to live with their maternal grandmother, Mary Livingston Ludlow Hall. She became their guardian and was responsible for taking care of them.

Theodore Roosevelt and his second wife, Edith, sit with their children on the lawn at Sagamore Hill in 1903; from left—Quentin, Ted, Archie, Alice, Kermit, and Ethel.

Although she frequently wrote to Elliott about his children's education and accomplishments, Mrs. Hall discouraged him from visiting.

Following the unexpected death of his young wife, Elliott started drinking again—and heavily. Grandmother Hall hoped to keep this information from his three children. However, Eleanor repeatedly questioned why she could not see her father.

Eleanor would later write of her childhood that she was taught to "do her duty." She added, "not my duty as I saw it, but my duty as laid down for me by other people." While life with Grandmother Hall was not always easy, Eleanor remained somewhat content.

Swept into the arms of her great, bearlike uncle, Eleanor knew she was deeply and genuinely loved.

At least once a year, she was invited to visit Uncle Ted (Theodore Roosevelt), Aunt Edith, and their children at their Sagamore Hill home. After one visit, Edith Roosevelt wrote to a family member, "Poor little soul, she is very plain. Her teeth and mouth seem to have no future. But the ugly duckling may turn out to be a swan." Both Aunt Edith and Uncle Ted were affectionate and loving toward Eleanor. These visits to Sagamore Hill provided a sense of family stability and refuge for Eleanor when she needed it the most. Swept into the arms of her great, bearlike uncle, Eleanor knew she was deeply and genuinely loved.

Whether at Grandmother Hall's Manhattan brownstone or at Oak Terrace, the Halls' summer home at Tivoli along the Hudson River in New York, Eleanor—under the watchful eyes of a somewhat bad-tempered French governess—would often retreat to the library and her imagination. During the months spent at

Oak Terrace each summer, there were rarely any children for Eleanor to play with. However, she could ride her pony, and her uncles taught her to ride a bicycle, both of which gave her some sense of freedom. Her happiest moments, she would write, were when she was alone "when no one would bother me."

Reading her father's infrequent letters, Eleanor dreamed of a future in which her family would be reunited. She wanted to take care of her heartsick father and two younger brothers. However, Elliott's continued attempts to stop drinking all failed; and in May of 1893, Eleanor's brother Elliott Jr. died from complications

In one of the last letters she would write to her father, Eleanor tells of an upcoming visit to Bar Harbor, Maine. Elliott's pet name for his daughter, "Little Nell," came from a character in a Charles Dickens story.

of scarlet fever and diphtheria. Learning the news of his youngest son's death, Elliott seemed to give up. Although letters to his beloved "little Nell" continued to mention a time when they would be together, this was not meant to be. Elliott died on August 14, 1894. He was only thirty-four. Eleanor, faithful to the end, was heartbroken. "My aunts told me, but I simply refused to believe it," she would later write. Grandmother Hall, hoping to spare the children further sadness, would not let Eleanor and Hall attend their father's funeral.

On Her Own

Private tutoring in subjects such as music, German, and French, along with lessons in dance and piano, filled the years ahead. When Eleanor's life had once been made up of upheaval and uncertainty, it now had routine and structure. When she was fifteen, her grandmother decided that Eleanor should be sent to Europe to continue her education. In her autobiography, Eleanor wrote that she felt as though she were "starting a new life." Accompanied on her journey across the Atlantic by her aunt Tissie—one of her mother's sisters— Eleanor was enrolled in the fall of 1899 at the Allenswood Academy, a girls' private school near London, England.

When Eleanor's life had once been made up of upheaval and uncertainty, it now had routine and structure.

At Allenswood, Eleanor blossomed. Nicknamed "Totty," she was popular with her fellow students and soon became a class leader. Eleanor also became a special favorite of Mademoiselle Marie Souvestre, the school's strong-willed, seventy-year-old headmistress.

Allenswood Academy

Located outside London, Allenswood Academy offered higher learning to the daughters of wealthy European and American families. Its founder and headmistress, Mademoiselle Marie Souvestre, was a dedicated **feminist**. She was the daughter of Émile Souvestre, a well-known French novelist and philosopher. At Allenswood, young women were taught to consider critical social issues while studying geography, literature, history, and foreign languages.

Marie Souvestre,
headmistress of
Allenswood Academy

In a culture that downplayed the education of women, Allenswood was unique. Classes were conducted entirely in French. Anyone who spoke English had to confess her error before entering the dining room. Baths were limited to ten minutes three times per week. Beds, closets, and bureaus were frequently inspected. Linens and personal possessions were dumped in a pile if not kept orderly. Dinner was formal, but there were occasional parties. Two hours were allotted each day for exercise. Despite the somewhat restrictive environment, students—such as Eleanor Roosevelt—thrived.

Marie Souvestre was known for her piercing gaze and strong convictions. A former student noted that participating in a discussion with the highly respected headmistress "was an education in itself."

Eleanor had hoped to remain at Allenswood for a fourth year. However, once she was eighteen, her Grandmother Hall beckoned from across the Atlantic. It was time for Eleanor's formal introduction to society—her debut. While she dreaded the prospect, to refuse would have been unthinkable. This was the end of Eleanor's formal education.

Eleanor (last row, circled) stands with fellow Allenswood students in 1900. Her three years at the exclusive all-girl's school marked the end of Eleanor's formal education.

Unlike many of the popular "finishing schools" of this period, Allenswood was more progressive. The school focused on teaching young women to think for themselves, instead of just how to run a household and be a successful wife and society hostess. Mademoiselle Souvestre took her duties as an educator of young women very seriously. Although French was spoken almost exclusively at Allenswood, Eleanor was at ease making conversation thanks to the childhood nanny who had taught her to speak the language fluently. Eleanor developed confidence and a personal sense of style and grace while she exercised her mind. At Allenswood, she participated in heated discussions about politics and world issues of the day. "Whatever I have become," Eleanor would later write in her autobiography, "had its seeds in those three years of contact with a liberal mind and strong personality."

Returning Home

The young woman who sailed back across the Atlantic in 1902 was a changed individual in a changed world. Family circumstances had altered as well, for Eleanor was now the niece of the president of the United States. Her uncle Ted assumed the office when his predecessor, William McKinley, had been struck down by an assassin's bullet the previous year.

The summer before Eleanor's debut was spent, once again, at Oak Terrace. By all accounts, it was not a happy time. Grandmother Hall remained closed up in her bedroom for hours at a time, with little social contact. Also, the unpredictable behavior of Eleanor's uncle Vallie—a serious alcoholic—made life nearly unbearable. On more than one occasion, he fired a rifle from an upstairs window at unsuspecting houseguests taking a stroll on the grounds. Eleanor would later write "that first summer was not good preparation for being a gay and joyous debutante."

Soon she was caught up in the many social obligations that a young woman of her age and social class was expected to attend.

But in the fall, Eleanor returned to her grandmother's Manhattan home. Soon she was caught up in the many social obligations that a young woman of her age and social class was expected to attend. She also began to take a more active role in the upbringing of her brother, Hall. Eleanor accompanied him to boarding school, arranged social activities and parties for him, and took him on trips. Only eighteen, Eleanor took this new responsibility very seriously. She never wanted Hall to feel the sense of abandonment and lack of family support that she had experienced.

Although perhaps not the famous beauty her mother was, Eleanor displayed a newfound maturity and poise. These features, when combined with her slim figure and brilliant pale blue eyes, were enough to attract the attention of more than a few admirers. Despite often feeling ill at ease and unattractive, Eleanor was by no means unpopular during the social season. Dressed in an elegant French gown, she made her formal debut at the Assembly Ball, held on December 11, 1902, at New York City's Waldorf-Astoria Hotel. Although later described by Eleanor as "utter agony," her entrance into society was undoubtedly a success. For Eleanor, perhaps the single brightest element in her life since she had returned from England was her deepening relationship with Franklin Delano Roosevelt, her attractive fifth cousin.

Eleanor, at age 18, poses for a portrait taken to mark her formal debut into society. She dreaded the seemingly endless round of parties and other social events, calling them "utter agony."

CHAPTER 3

For Better or Worse

It was a wife's duty to be interested in whatever interested her husband, whether it was politics, books, or a particular dish for dinner.

About the time of her 1902 debut, Eleanor became a member of the Junior League of New York. This relatively new organization was formed by young society women interested in community service. While some Junior League members simply chose to donate money, Eleanor chose a more hands-on approach. She began performing social work among Manhattan's immigrant population. She taught dance and exercise classes to young children at the College Settlement on Rivington Street on New York City's Lower East Side. Eleanor enjoyed the gaiety and enthusiasm of the children, many of whom came to class after completing twelve- to sixteen-hour factory shifts.

In the early 1800s, 30 percent of the workforce in U.S. factories was made up of children ages seven to twelve. By 1910, some two million children under the age of fifteen worked for wages. Easily managed and difficult to organize into unions, children were paid less than adults and were required to perform tasks

As early as 1912, Eleanor Roosevelt had actively supported the fight against child labor.

Child Labor in the United States

Child labor has been common practice since colonial times, but it evolved during the nineteenth century from helping on the family farm to backbreaking factory work under terrible conditions.

By the mid- to late-nineteenth century, reformers began to press for legislation that would protect younger workers. For the most part, working conditions were slow to improve. Children were maimed or killed while using dangerous equipment. Many suffered from work-related health problems. Eventually, some states set minimum requirements for school attendance, ensuring children at least a primary school education. By 1900, twenty-four states had set minimum-age requirements for children working in factories. In 1904, the National Child Labor Committee, a private institution, was formed to seek the abolishment of child labor.

Young worker in West Virginia coal mine, 1908.

As early as 1912, Eleanor Roosevelt had actively supported the fight against child labor. During her husband's term as governor of New York, Eleanor testified in favor of labor reforms. Victory was finally attained with the passage of the Fair Labor Standards Act in 1938. This legislation not only prohibited all child labor, but also set a minimum-wage standard and established a forty-hour work-week for adults.

that were often unappealing, unsanitary, and unsafe.

Eleanor also joined the Consumers League in 1903. This group investigated employment conditions and wages of young women workers. Eleanor and her fellow League members participated in inspections of department stores and garment factories. A sense of duty and obligation to less fortunate people had always been stressed by Eleanor's family throughout her childhood. When she was very young, she had gone to the Children's Aid Society with family members to help serve Christmas dinner there. Social responsibility was further stressed at Allenswood by Mademoiselle Souvestre. Eleanor later described herself as somewhat innocent and unsophisticated at that point in her life but also as someone who knew a lot about "some of the less agreeable sides of life."

Earlier in 1902, just after she had returned from England, Eleanor was traveling by train from New York City northward to Grandmother Hall's summer home at Tivoli. Also on the train, but in another car, was Franklin Roosevelt, who was heading to his family home in Hyde Park with his mother. Franklin had just finished his sophomore year at Harvard. While walking through the train to stretch his legs, Franklin spotted Eleanor. Even

Franklin D. Roosevelt, aged 18 months, sits perched on the shoulder of his father. James Roosevelt instilled in his son a lifelong love of sports and the outdoors.

though the two cousins had not seen each other in several years, they felt very comfortable with each other and began a friendly conversation.

Franklin was the only child of James and Sara Roosevelt. James, like Eleanor's father, Elliott, was also a descendent of Nicholas Roosevelt. In the spring of 1880, James was a wealthy widower living the relatively peaceful life of a country squire at Springwood, his 600-acre home along the Hudson River in Hyde Park. Attending a small dinner party in New York City, he met the beautiful Sara Delano. She was twenty-six—nearly half his age. Both fell in love. Six months later they wed, and soon departed on a lengthy ten-month European honeymoon. On January 30, 1882, Sara gave birth to their son—Franklin Delano Roosevelt.

Unlike Eleanor's, Franklin's childhood was a happy one. Although James Roosevelt suffered from ill health for several years and died when Franklin was only eighteen, he still spent many precious hours with his son. James taught Franklin to ride, fish, shoot, sail, hunt, and much more. Sara Roosevelt, too, was devoted to Franklin and provided a supportive and loving home environment. When her husband died, the wealthy forty-six-year-old widow turned all her attention to her only child. Franklin would continue to be his mother's focal point for the rest of her life.

Courtship and Love

After the chance meeting on the train, the two cousins saw each other more and more often over the coming months. Eleanor had known Franklin's mother for many years, and she affectionately called her "Cousin Sally." Eleanor was invited to Hyde Park and to the Roosevelts' summer home on Campobello Island in New Brunswick, Canada, near the Maine coast. Eleanor and Franklin also sometimes met for lunch or tea, and both

Twelve-year-old Franklin stands with his mother, Sara in 1893. Daughter of a wealthy New York merchant, Sara Delano Roosevelt was devoted to her only son.

attended a New Year's reception given by Theodore Roosevelt at the White House.

Sometimes Franklin would escort Eleanor home from her volunteer work at the College Settlement on Rivington Street. These firsthand looks at poverty and unhealthy living conditions were eye-openers for Franklin, who commented, "I could not believe human beings lived that way." Through Eleanor, Franklin got his first real introduction to a world that was entirely different from his own. The more committed Eleanor became to Franklin, the more she felt it was important to show him the things in life that mattered to her. A granddaughter later wrote of Eleanor, "This was a woman who thought about things, who had opinions, who had developed an intellect, was well read, and wasn't afraid to talk about her opinions and her feelings. And this was quite uncommon for many of the young women FDR had known." Franklin was captivated.

During their courtship, Eleanor and Franklin were expected to follow the rigid social rules of the Victorian era. Young women were strictly chaperoned, and young couples were never allowed to be alone together. If a relative wasn't available, a maid would serve as a companion. Young women were not allowed to express interest in a specific man—it was up to the man to make the first contact. No letters or notes were allowed unless, Eleanor wrote, "you knew a man very well." The use of first names was also frowned upon, and the only acceptable presents from a man to a woman were candy, flowers, or perhaps a book (depending on the subject matter, of course). A young woman, not married or engaged, who accepted a piece

Standing tall, Franklin Roosevelt (center, with arms crossed) poses with other members of Harvard's Class of 1904 on Nantasket Beach, near Boston.

A young and playful Franklin and Eleanor laugh on the grounds of Algonac, the Delano family country estate in New York's Hudson River Valley.

of jewelry from an admirer was viewed as having loose morals. Physical demonstrations, such as modest kisses, were definitely not acceptable until after a couple was engaged. The rules were inflexible, and those courting were expected to follow them.

By the fall of 1903, Franklin had made up his mind; he asked Eleanor to marry him. "It seemed," she later wrote, "an entirely natural thing," for the two had more in common than many people realized. Both had been raised in homes where there was little contact with others their own age. They were fifth cousins, and their families—though not closely related—were good friends. When Sara and James Roosevelt had sailed to Europe on their honeymoon in 1880, Elliott Roosevelt was on the same ship about to begin his own around-the-world travels.

James and Sara were so fond of Elliott that they later asked him to serve as godfather to their baby son. Eleanor and Franklin had known each other—though not well—for many years.

Although Eleanor answered yes on that autumn day, "it was years later," she wrote in her autobiography, "before I understood what being in love or what loving really meant." Sara Roosevelt, taken by surprise, was not happy. She felt the couple was too young for such a monumental step and asked that they keep their engagement a secret for a year. In a letter sent by Franklin to his mother from Harvard in December of 1903, he wrote: "Dearest Mama—I know what pain I must have caused you and you know I wouldn't do it if I really could have helped it.... [Y]ou know that nothing can ever change what we have always been and always will be to each other—only now you have two children to love and to love you—and Eleanor as you know will always be a daughter to you in every true way. Your ever loving, FDR."

Through Eleanor, Franklin got his first real introduction to a world that was entirely different from his own.

Throughout the year that followed, Eleanor and Franklin's feelings for each other only deepened. Sara gave in, and their engagement was formally announced in November of 1904. Upon hearing the news of his niece's engagement, Theodore Roosevelt wrote immediately to Eleanor, "Dear girl, I rejoice deeply in your happiness."

Uncle Ted

Writer, naturalist, soldier, and statesman, Theodore Roosevelt (1858–1919) was a hero of the Spanish-American War and the twenty-sixth president of the United States. After holding a series of elected and appointed political positions, Roosevelt served as vice president under William McKinley. Roosevelt took over the office of president when McKinley was killed by an assassin's bullet in 1901. At forty-two, he became the youngest man ever to serve as a U.S. president.

The Roosevelt administration's foreign policy was reflected in the popular phrase "Speak softly, and carry a big stick." His efforts at helping to obtain peace during the Russo-Japanese War earned Theodore Roosevelt the Nobel Prize in 1906. Other accomplishments of the Roosevelt presidency included constructing the Panama Canal; beginning the U.S. Forest Service; and the setting aside of five national parks, 150 national forests, and fifty-one wildlife refuges.

After leaving the White House in 1909, Roosevelt went on an African safari. In 1912, he tried to run for president again but was unsuccessful. He ran as a candidate of the Progressive—or Bull Moose—Party (from Roosevelt's comment, "I am as strong as a bull moose"). Returning to private life, he wrote his autobiography, continued to travel, and still kept track of national politics. Roosevelt died at his home, Sagamore Hill, on January 6, 1919.

Roosevelt's first wife, Alice, died shortly after the birth of their only child—a daughter. He and his second wife, Edith, had five children.

Theodore Roosevelt and his Rough Riders stand atop Cuba's San Juan Hill, 1888.

Franklin's Wife

Wearing her mother's veil and her mother-in-law's pearls, Eleanor married Franklin on March 17, 1905—on what would have been Anna Hall Roosevelt's forty-second birthday. The date had been selected to accommodate the presidential schedule, as Uncle Ted was participating in New York City's annual St. Patrick's Day parade before walking his niece down the aisle.

In the candlelit drawing room of Eleanor's aunt, the couple stood beneath an arrangement of roses and palms and said their vows in front of about two hundred guests. The distant strains of "The Wearin' o' the Green" could be heard from the street outside, where St. Patrick's Day celebrations were still going on. After the ceremony, Theodore Roosevelt remarked, "Well, Franklin, there's nothing like keeping the name in the family!"

Because the president was in attendance, an article about the wedding made the front page of *The New York Times*.

There were no photographs taken of the wedding ceremony and reception, as was the custom of the day. The only photo of Eleanor in her wedding gown was taken at a studio some time earlier. Franklin's gift to his bride was a small gold pin that incorporated the Roosevelt

No photographs were taken at Eleanor's wedding to Franklin, but Sara Roosevelt arranged to have this studio portrait taken several weeks beforehand.

family crest of three roses and three feather plumes. Earlier, as Eleanor was dressing upstairs, a telegram had arrived from England. It contained just one word, *Bonheur* ("Happiness"). The message was from Eleanor's beloved friend and former headmistress, Marie Souvestre, who, sadly, died from cancer less than two weeks later.

After a week alone together at Hyde Park (Sara had remained in Manhattan), Eleanor and Franklin returned to the city and moved into a small apartment so that Franklin could finish that term's classes at Columbia University. At the beginning of the summer, they left for a three-month-long European honeymoon. They were mistaken for the *Theodore* Roosevelts in London and were given the royal suite in a hotel. Among their other stops were Paris, Switzerland, Scotland, Germany, and Italy where, Eleanor noted, "Franklin refused to look at any more churches."

One of several engagement photos taken of Eleanor in 1904; she was 20 years old. The motherless Eleanor shopped for her wedding finery with her cousin, Susie Parish, whose family hosted the ceremony at their home.

Upon their return from Europe, Eleanor learned that her recent ill health had not been seasickness but something else entirely. She was pregnant with their first child. Franklin resumed his law studies, and the newlyweds settled into a rented Manhattan brownstone located just three blocks from Franklin's mother. Sara Roosevelt had personally selected, furnished, and staffed the house for them. In the early years of her marriage, Eleanor—perhaps remembering the lack of closeness she had experienced with her own mother—tried hard to forge a loving

In the Name of the Father, and of the Son, and of the Holy Ghost, Amen.

Diocese of New York.

Church of the Incarnation, New York City.

✝

This is to Certify

That Franklin Delano Roosevelt

and Eleanor Roosevelt

were united in

Holy Matrimony

According to the Rite of the Protestant Episcopal Church in the United States of America, and the Laws of the State of New York, on this Seventeenth day of March A.D. 1905.

Endicott Peabody, Rector.

Witnesses.

Theodore Roosevelt
Edith Kermit Roosevelt

What therefore God hath joined together let not man put asunder.—St. Mark x. 9

Eleanor and Franklin's marriage certificate—Theodore and Edith Roosevelt, the president and first lady, signed as witnesses to the ceremony.

At one stop on the couple's three-month-long European honeymoon, Franklin snapped this photo of Eleanor sitting in a Venetian gondola holding his hat.

and strong bond with Sara. For the motherless, insecure, twenty-year-old Eleanor, Sara Roosevelt would become perhaps the single greatest female influence throughout her young adulthood.

CHAPTER 4

Years of Change

*People grow through experience
if they meet life honestly and courageously.
This is how character is built.*

In the spring of 1906, Eleanor gave birth to Anna, the first of six children, "For ten years," she later wrote, "I was always just getting over having a baby or about to have one." After graduating from Harvard in 1904, Franklin had begun law studies at New York's Columbia University. By the time Anna was born he had finished his requirements for law school and passed the bar exam—a series of tests that determine whether or not an individual is qualified to practice law. He then began work as an unpaid **apprentice** clerk in a Wall Street law firm. Unlike the immigrant families living elsewhere in the city, the Roosevelts did not worry about financial security. At the time of their marriage, Eleanor and Franklin's combined annual income

Twenty-one-year-old Eleanor
holds her first child—and only daughter—
Anna Eleanor Roosevelt, in 1906.

from family investments amounted to about $250,000 in today's dollars.

With the arrival of a second child, James, in December of 1907, Eleanor—at her mother-in-law's urging—gave up most of her volunteer work. "As young women go," Eleanor later wrote, "I suppose I was fitting pretty well into the pattern of a fairly conventional, quiet, young society matron." Sara Roosevelt's Christmas gift to the growing family was a spacious new home she was having built for them in Manhattan. There was just one drawback—another house was under construction next door. This twin would be Sara's new home, and the two buildings would be connected by sliding doors on nearly every floor. Once the two households were settled, it was impossible to know, wrote Eleanor of her mother-in-law, "when she would appear, night or day."

After the sadness of her childhood, more than anything Eleanor wanted the love and security of a happy family life.

In the early years of her marriage Eleanor was caught in a difficult emotional situation. On one hand, she wanted to please both her husband and her mother-in-law. Many times she kept quiet when something happened that upset her. After the sadness of her childhood, more than anything Eleanor wanted the love and security of a happy family life. With no experience in running a household, managing servants, or raising children, Eleanor looked to Sara for guidance and support in all of these areas. On the other hand, turning to Sara increased Eleanor's lack of self-confidence. The children, too, learned to go to their grandmother instead of their mother when they wanted something. The more Eleanor turned to Sara, the less she felt she could do things on her own. With time, resentful feelings began to stir and grow in Eleanor.

In 1909, Sara also purchased a summer cottage for her son and his family on Campobello Island. Unlike the twin Manhattan townhouses, this structure was set apart. But Sara's house was close by—just to the north on the other side of a privet hedge. Eleanor considered this cottage her first real home. Here, she could decorate as she chose.

By this time, Eleanor was expecting her third child. Franklin Jr. was born on March 18, 1909. The baby's proud mother noted that he was "the biggest and most beautiful of all the babies." Although healthy at first, the infant died during a flu outbreak

Franklin's mother, Sara Roosevelt (at left), talks with Eleanor during a visit to the family's summer home on Campobello Island, off the coast of Maine.

Summers at "Campo" were a Roosevelt family tradition. Outdoor activities included hiking, fishing, boating, and tennis. Eleanor (top center) and Franklin (bottom center) pose with guests in this 1910 photo.

just seven months later. It was a terrible loss. Eleanor blamed herself for the baby's death, questioning whether there was something she could have done to prevent it. "My heart aches for Eleanor," wrote Sara in her diary. Eleanor remained depressed for months. New happiness came to Eleanor and Franklin in September 1910, when another son—Elliott—was born.

To Albany and Beyond

By this time, Franklin had grown restless and bored with the law. A seat was available in the New York State Senate, and Democratic Party leaders from the Hyde Park area encouraged him to run. Traveling more than two thousand miles over upstate

New York roads, the twenty-eight-year-old candidate was the first in the area to campaign by car. The time seemed ripe for change, and Franklin won an upset victory in 1910. Franklin took on the job of state senator and moved his growing family to the state capital in Albany, where the Roosevelts rented a house.

For Eleanor, life in Albany offered a break from living next door to her mother-in-law. "For the first time I was going to live on my own," Eleanor wrote years later. "I wanted to be independent. I was beginning to realize that something within me craved to be an individual." Fulfilling her role as a young politician's wife, Eleanor attended teas and made social calls. The Roosevelt home became a popular meeting place for those in Franklin's political circle. Eleanor listened and learned and what had once been just a spark of interest in politics burned more brightly. Away from Sara, with more opportunities to share in Franklin's world, Eleanor sensed the beginnings of a transformation. However, with three very young children at home, family life was still the center of her existence.

Franklin Roosevelt addresses a crowd in Dutchess County, New York, during his first run for political office. His campaign a success, Franklin was elected to the state senate in 1910.

When not with his family, Franklin was busy with his state senate re-election campaign. To help manage the operation, Franklin hired a well-known newspaper reporter, Louis Howe, as his personal assistant. After serving very successfully as a state senator in Albany, Franklin found opportunity knocking once again two years later in 1913, when he was appointed to serve as assistant secretary of the navy in President Woodrow Wilson's administration. Both positions—in the New York State Senate and at the Department of the Navy—had also been held by Theodore Roosevelt, whose political path to the White House was one Franklin hoped someday to follow.

Franklin's job change meant a relocation to Washington, D.C. With frequent trips to Hyde Park, Manhattan, and Campobello Island already part of their routine, travel was a constant in the life of the Roosevelt family. It was up to Eleanor to coordinate each move, making sure no children, staff, pets, or personal belongings were left behind. When the family traveled, said a friend, it was like "an army on the move."

Travel was a constant in the life of the Roosevelt family. It was up to Eleanor to coordinate each move.

Life in Washington meant even more extensive social obligations for Eleanor. She was expected to host and attend a variety of functions, call on the wives of other officials (making sometimes as many as sixty such calls in a week), answer notes and letters, and—of course—oversee the smooth running of her household. Feeling somewhat overwhelmed, she hired a social secretary to assist her. Born into a socially prominent Catholic family from Maryland that had fallen on hard times, Lucy Mercer seemed the perfect choice. The energetic twenty-two-year-old

Louis Howe

Making a good first impression did not seem high on the priority list of Louis McHenry Howe (1871–1936). Frail, often suffering from health problems, his wrinkled clothes dusted with cigarette ashes, Howe described himself as "one of the four ugliest men in the State of New York." An experienced newspaper reporter with strong political connections, Howe became the manager of Franklin Roosevelt's state senate re-election campaign in 1912. It marked the beginning of a relationship that would span nearly a quarter century.

"I was so impressed with Franklin Roosevelt," related Howe after their first meeting, "I made up my mind that he was presidential timber and that nothing but an accident could keep him from becoming president of the United States."

Eleanor Roosevelt's first reaction to Howe was not favorable. "I was as determined that I would not like him as he was that I should," she later wrote. However, Howe began a careful campaign of persistence—seeking Eleanor out, asking for her comments on her husband's speeches, and listening to her opinions on important issues. Soon she began to appreciate his strengths.

After Franklin Roosevelt was elected governor of New York, Howe began to coordinate behind-the-scene efforts to secure FDR's presidential nomination. Once in the White House, Howe's title would be personal secretary and would grant him unlimited access to the president.

Following Howe's death in 1936, Eleanor would describe him as "one of the seven most important people" in her life.

Eleanor and Franklin relax on the beach at Campobello after a family picnic in 1910. Both loved the island's salty breezes and peaceful solitude.

was invaluable in helping Eleanor learn about the details of Washington society. "She is so sweet and attractive and adores you, Eleanor," wrote Sara after meeting the young woman. Eleanor appreciated Lucy's help even more during the summer of 1914 as she was expecting yet another child. The Roosevelt's fifth child was born in August at Campobello. Also named Franklin Delano Roosevelt Jr., *this* child would remain healthy and strong.

By the summer of 1914, Europe was at war—though the United States would not join in the conflict until April 6, 1917. At the Department of the Navy, Franklin spent those three years building up the stocks of goods and supplies directed to naval bases and factories and preparing for the possibility of war. When it came, the navy was ready. By the war's end, the number of commissioned ships had grown from 197 to more than 2,000, and its naval forces had increased from 65,000 to nearly a half million men.

Wartime Volunteer

Eleanor gave birth to her final child, John, in the spring of 1916. She now found herself more confident in her role as a parent. With the three older children in school and Lucy Mercer by her side to help with social obligations, Eleanor decided to resume her volunteer work in 1918. This time, she focused her energies on the war effort. At the American Red Cross canteen located in Washington's Union Station, Eleanor took on just about any job—be it serving free hot meals or scrubbing floors. Through the Navy League, she supervised about forty knitters. She was also often found at a local hospital visiting wounded soldiers and sailors. Some mornings she would get up at five a.m. to handle her volunteer work; some evenings she would arrive

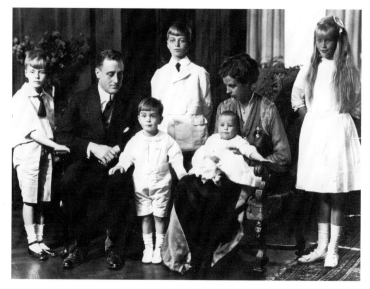

Franklin and Eleanor pose with their children in 1916. From left are Elliott, Franklin, Jr., James, John (on his mother's lap), and Anna.

home after midnight. Although Eleanor had originally taken all of this work on out of a sense of duty, she found that—despite the long hours—these accomplishments made her feel very good. A friend recalled that World War I "pushed Eleanor Roosevelt into the first real work *outside her family* since she was married twelve years before."

The Roosevelt children spent most of the summer of 1918 with their grandmother in Hyde Park. Eleanor made frequent visits but continued her duties in Washington with the Red Cross. That same summer, like many other women of the day, Eleanor also learned to drive a car. Eleanor and Franklin's absence took a toll on their children. James, the oldest Roosevelt son, writing later about his mother, said "most of her children were reared more by their grandmother and by maids and nannies than by their mother. Meanwhile, father was too busy building his political career to play a regular role in our upbringing."

Eleanor decided to resume her volunteer work in 1918. This time, she focused her energies on the war effort.

In July, Franklin headed to Europe on an inspection tour of U.S. naval facilities. Traveling in France and Britain, he had a firsthand look at combat areas and battlefields. The horrible devastation Franklin viewed would remain in his memory for the rest of his life. Sailing home in September, after the grueling tour, he developed double pneumonia and influenza. Notified by telegram of Franklin's condition, Sara and Eleanor met his ship at its dock in New York with an ambulance and a doctor in attendance.

British soldiers fight from a trench during the Battle of the Somme in 1916. When the U.S. joined in the fight the following year, Eleanor signed on as a Red Cross volunteer.

During the time Eleanor remained in New York to help care for her ailing husband, she made a life-changing discovery. While unpacking Franklin's luggage, she came across a packet of love letters addressed to her husband from Lucy Mercer. Eleanor was wounded as she faced hard evidence of betrayal by yet another person she loved. "I think the greatest hurt was that Franklin had broken his word," said a family friend. "It was like her father, who had made promises and not kept them."

Thirty-four years old, with five children under the age of thirteen, Eleanor offered her husband a divorce—a scandalous option for people of their background. Franklin hesitated. Lucy Mercer was a Catholic and the Church forbade her marrying a divorced man. Louis Howe, Franklin's trusted advisor, warned him that a bid for the White House would be out of the question if Franklin were to divorce his wife. And Sara Roosevelt, firmly in control of the majority of the family purse strings, warned that she would cut her son off financially if he left Eleanor and his children. Franklin, still caring for Eleanor, bowed by guilt, and concerned for his political future, agreed never to see Lucy Mercer again. Yet the marriage of Eleanor and Franklin had changed forever. In the future, theirs would be a partnership based upon caring and respect, but Eleanor would not entrust her heart to Franklin again. "I have the memory of an elephant," she wrote many years later. "I can forgive but I can never forget."

Young and beautiful, Lucy Mercer was Eleanor's social secretary. Eleanor's discovery in 1917 of Franklin's affair with Lucy would forever alter the Roosevelt's marriage.

CHAPTER 5

Beating the Odds

You must do the things you think you cannot do.

Although her marriage had remained intact despite the near-fatal blow of discovering Franklin's romance with Lucy Mercer, Eleanor later reflected that "the bottom dropped out of my own particular world and I faced myself, my surroundings, my world honestly for the first time." The effects were long-term and long-lasting. At some point during this period, Eleanor destroyed all the love letters sent to her by Franklin during their courtship.

Once cherished, this correspondence now seemed another form of betrayal. The timid young woman, who was used to obeying her husband and mother-in-law, was gradually replaced by someone who stood her ground and made her own decisions.

In the years to come, the marriage of Eleanor and Franklin changed into more of an **alliance** between two individuals with

Franklin and Eleanor sit quietly together on the porch of Springwood, the Roosevelt family home in Hyde Park, New York. Their relationship had changed from a romance to a partnership.

great admiration and respect for each other. Their son Elliott later wrote of his parents' marriage, "It became a very close and very intimate partnership of great affection—never in a physical sense, but in a tremendously mental sense. But there were very few light moments. ."

In January 1919, Eleanor and Franklin set sail for Europe. It was their first trip abroad together since their honeymoon nearly fifteen years earlier. While they were at sea, sad news arrived by telegraph: Uncle Ted had died in his sleep at Sagamore Hill after an illness.

Once in Europe, it was Franklin's responsibility—as assistant secretary of the navy—to supervise the dismantling and distribution of postwar military property and supplies. During these weeks in Europe, Eleanor saw the devastation of the war as she toured the countryside with her husband. Endless roads of thick mud were edged and crisscrossed with bombshell holes. Piles of stones—some holding hand-lettered signs stuck on posts—were all that remained of towns destroyed by bombings. Entire forests were reduced to hillsides of stumps. Everywhere there were signs of destruction and death. Deeply affected by all they had seen, the Roosevelts sailed for home in mid-February. On the same ship were President and Mrs. Wilson, who were returning from the Paris Peace Conference with news of the recently formed **League of Nations**.

The timid young woman, who was used to obeying her husband and mother-in-law, was gradually replaced by someone who stood her ground and made her own decisions.

Even though the war was now over, Eleanor was still very

The scenes of devastation and destruction that Franklin and Eleanor witnessed during their 1919 visit to postwar Europe would haunt them both forever.

active as a volunteer. In 1919, she encouraged Secretary of the Interior Franklin Lane to investigate conditions at Washington, D.C.'s St. Elizabeth's Hospital. The country's only federal facility for the mentally ill, St. Elizabeth's housed a number of traumatized war veterans. In the course of her work with the Navy League, Eleanor had visited the hospital and had been shocked by what she saw. As a result of her persistent efforts, much-needed Congressional funding was provided for improving conditions there.

Greater Things

In 1920, Franklin made the decision to enter national politics. That summer, after resigning his Department of the Navy post, he was chosen as James Cox's vice-presidential running mate. "I was glad for my husband," Eleanor wrote, "but it never occurred to me to be much excited." Initially, Eleanor felt unwelcome in the national political arena. These feelings contributed to her lack of interest. However, the upcoming presidential election was the first in which women would be allowed to vote and being a candidate's wife suddenly carried more importance.

At her husband's request, Eleanor joined Franklin on his campaign train, dutifully smiling at his side as he spoke to audiences in more than thirty states. As the only woman among the aides and newspapermen in Franklin's campaign circle, Eleanor felt like an outsider looking in. However, Louis Howe made a point of seeking her out and stirring her interest in Franklin's vice-presidential bid. It was at this time that Louis Howe's friendship with Eleanor firmly took root. Based on their common ground of support for Franklin, this unlikely bond would become invaluable in the future.

Suffragists picket in front of the White House in 1917. Three years later, twenty-six million women—half the country's population—would finally be given the right to vote.

Although the Cox-Roosevelt ticket was defeated, it had brought important national recognition for Franklin. Even though he was returning to private life, Franklin continued to make plans for greater things. Eleanor, on the other hand, did not look forward to moving back to New York City and a life of seemingly endless teas, luncheons, and dinners. Yet somehow she was able to keep a foot in two different worlds—one of wealth and privilege into which she had been born and the other of activism and reform in which she was now very interested. She took business courses—such as shorthand and typing—and

The National League of Women Voters was founded in 1920 to promote international women's suffrage and participation in government. That same year, members pose with a placard outlining their political platform.

joined the newly established League of Women Voters. Rising rapidly through that organization's ranks, Eleanor chaired their Legislative Affairs Committee and helped to draft policy. In early 1921, she attended the league's national **convention** in Chicago. Soon Franklin's was not the only Roosevelt name in the news. *The New York Times* referred to Eleanor as a woman of influence "who speaks her political mind."

In the summer of 1921, as they did each year, the Roosevelt family headed for their home on Campobello Island for days of fishing, sailing, riding, swimming, hiking, and picnicking. One afternoon in August, after an especially active day, Franklin complained of chills and tiredness. By the following morning, fever and paralysis had set in.

Misdiagnosed for nearly two weeks as a bad cold and then as a blood clot on the spinal column, the illness was finally identified by a specialist. The news was grim. Franklin had infantile paralysis—polio— a disease for which there was then no known cure or treatment. Franklin's life, and Eleanor's, had changed forever.

Eleanor and Franklin pause on the beach at Campobello. After being stricken with polio in the summer of 1921, Franklin would never stand again without assistance.

No Turning Back

Louis Howe and his family had been visiting the Roosevelts when Franklin fell ill. During the first few weeks—before Franklin was moved to a New York City hospital—Louis Howe shared with Eleanor the tasks of bathing, moving, and caring for Franklin. The children knew something frightening had happened to their father, yet Elliott recalled "when we children were allowed a glimpse of him through the doorway, he grinned and struggled to gasp out a word or two in answer to our weepy 'hellos.' He wanted to ease our fears, no matter what his own were."

Sara Roosevelt rushed home from a trip to Europe and immediately traveled to her son's side. After visiting Franklin and seeing the extent of his paralysis, Sara encouraged her son to give up politics and return to Hyde Park to live out his life as a country gentleman. With the support of Louis Howe, Eleanor stood up to her mother-in-law and urged her husband to continue with his political plans. Franklin, confident that he would make a full recovery, sided with Eleanor. Louis Howe then moved into the Roosevelt's Manhattan home to manage Franklin's affairs and plan a strategy for his political future.

"He wanted to ease our fears, no matter what his own were."

As Franklin struggled with **rehabilitation** efforts, Louis Howe helped keep the Roosevelt name in the news by writing articles that listed Franklin as the author—a practice known as ghostwriting. He also urged and coached Eleanor to take on the role of her husband's "stand-in." By this time, she had had enough political experience of her own to help make a difference. Working with Eleanor on her public speaking, Howe "sat at the back of the audience," she later wrote, "and gave me pointers on what I should say and how I should say it. I had a bad habit, because I was nervous, of laughing when there was nothing to laugh at. He broke me of that…. His advice was: 'Have something you want to say, say it, and sit down.'"

In 1922, Eleanor joined the Women's Trade Union League. This liberal organization supported better working conditions for women and promoted the women's labor movement. She

Wearing custom-made "knickerbocker" trousers and a tweed jacket, Eleanor poses with friends Marion Dickerman (right), Nancy Cook (near left) and Marion's sister, Peggy Levenson (far left) on 1926 camping trip.

also began to write articles for various journals and magazines, such as "Why I Am a Democrat" for the *Junior League Bulletin*. She would also eventually serve as editor at the *Women's Democratic News*. Eleanor joined the Women's Division of New York's Democratic State Committee. She also began her long-standing friendship with the activists Marion Dickerman and Nancy Cook. Working to organize Democratic women throughout New York State, Eleanor campaigned for Al Smith in his bid for governor. In the midst of all her political activity, Eleanor also took time to act as both mother and father to her children—especially to the boys, who strongly missed outings with their once athletically gifted father.

As the months passed, Franklin continued to work determinedly on his rehabilitation—still hoping for a miracle. Eventually, he was fitted with steel braces that, when locked at the knees, enabled him to stand erect. Extending from hip to foot, each brace weighed five pounds. Leaning heavily on the arm of an escort, with crutches or canes in hand, Franklin was able to swing his body awkwardly forward. This effort took an enormous amount of physical strength.

Behind the scenes, Franklin's struggle to cope with his disability was tremendous. To change virtually overnight

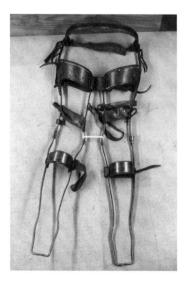

When locked in place, leg braces—made of leather and steel and weighing about 10 pounds—enabled Franklin to stand erect.

Disability and Deception

Convinced that his political career would come to an immediate end if the public knew the true extent of his paralysis, Franklin Roosevelt went to great lengths to conceal his limitations. At a time when most people were highly prejudiced against those with physical disabilities, Franklin made sure he was always photographed sitting in a car or in a regular chair or upright—with his braces locked—holding onto a speaker's platform or an aide's arm. Public appearances were always carefully staged in advance. His trousers were tailored so that they were long enough to cover most of his braces. His wheelchair was an armless kitchen chair modified to his specifications. Less noticeable, the chair was narrow enough to allow Franklin to easily maneuver it in tight spots.

A crutch and wheelchair used by Franklin following his paralysis stand in his Hyde Park bedroom closet.

Members of the press were willing participants in this deception. News agencies of the time honored the unwritten rule that Franklin never be photographed being carried or lifted. "No sob stuff," he requested in 1928. Although he fell in public at least three times, these occasions were never reported. Cartoons and caricatures usually depicted him running, standing, or leaping. Of the approximately 35,000 photographs of Franklin Roosevelt that exist today, there are only two that show him seated in a wheelchair, and they were never published.

from being an active man, constantly on the go, a lover of sports and the outdoors, to a helpless invalid must have seemed nearly unbearable. At one point, he asked Louis Howe why God had deserted him.

Franklin could not dress or undress himself without help. He could not get in or out of a bed or a car. He could not even

Delegates at the 1924 Democratic Convention, held at New York's Madison Square Garden, listen as Franklin Roosevelt nominates Al Smith for president. This event was Franklin's first major post-polio public appearance.

use the bathroom alone. If he dropped something on the floor, someone else would have to pick it up. Fearing the possibility of being trapped in a fire, Franklin spent hours practicing pulling himself across the floor with his arms—dragging his useless legs behind him. However, once Franklin had made the conscious decision not to retire from public life, his determination was strong. The public saw the confident, smiling man—not his white-knuckled grip on the podium or his sweat-drenched clothes or the strain caused by the physical effort of simply *living*.

Franklin made his first public appearance after being stricken by polio at the 1924 Democratic Convention. Holding tightly to the arm of his sixteen-year-old son, James, Franklin struggled to the podium. Once there, he gripped the lectern and captured his audience with a stirring speech nominating Al Smith for president. The crowd erupted in applause. Although

> *"No matter whether Governor Smith wins or loses, Franklin D. Roosevelt stands out as the real hero of the Democratic Convention of 1924."*

Smith would not succeed in his bid for higher office, Franklin's speech—in which he referred to the candidate as "the Happy Warrior of the political battlefield"—brought about a standing ovation. The *New York Herald Tribune* wrote "No matter whether Governor Smith wins or loses, Franklin D. Roosevelt stands out as the real hero of the Democratic Convention of 1924." Through his own grit and determination; the skillful strategic planning of his able friend and manager, Louis Howe; and the newly acquired political abilities of his wife, Eleanor, Franklin Roosevelt was back in the political game and ready for the next round.

Campobello

Located near the northern coast of Maine, in the Bay of Fundy, the Canadian island of Campobello was a popular vacation retreat for wealthy families at the turn of the last century. After a family visit to the area in 1883, when Franklin was just a year old, James Roosevelt purchased a home to use in the summer months. It was at Campobello that Franklin learned to sail and developed his lifelong love of ships and the sea.

Eleanor Roosevelt first visited the island in 1903 as a guest of Franklin and his mother. She, too, came to love Campobello's temperate summer climate and breathtaking coastal scenery. After their marriage, Eleanor and Franklin returned each summer with their growing family. In 1909, Sara Roosevelt purchased a wooden cottage with five acres located near her own summer home as a gift to her son and daughter-in-law. An addition to the cottage, constructed in 1915, expanded the structure to its present size of thirty-four rooms—of which eighteen are bedrooms and six are bathrooms. Conditions were somewhat primitive—there was no electricity or telephone, and lighting was provided by kerosene lanterns. Water was pumped from an outside well to third-floor storage tanks. Then gravity carried running water throughout the house. Seven fireplaces and a kitchen stove were the only sources of heat.

In 1964, the home became part of what is now the 2,800-acre Roosevelt-Campobello International Park.

Franklin sails his 45-foot schooner, the *Amberjack II*, in the waters off Campobello Island.

CHAPTER 6

The Road to Higher Office

Campaign behavior for wives: Always be on time.
Do as little talking as humanly possible.
Lean back in the parade car so everybody can
see the President.

Although his "Happy Warrior" speech marked the return of Franklin Roosevelt to the political arena, four years passed before he ran for public office again. In the period between the 1924 convention and 1928—when Al Smith and other New York State Democrats persuaded Franklin to run for governor, Eleanor and Franklin generally went their separate ways but continued a relationship of mutual respect and affection.

Eleanor began to feel truly needed, appreciated, and above all, *useful*. Her support of Franklin—physically, psychologically, and politically—had made the difference. Rather than returning to Hyde Park as an invalid, Franklin was ready to resume the challenges of public life. Facing his paralysis, he learned more compassion for less fortunate people and developed a greater sensitivity toward others. Passing through the twin ordeals of the Lucy Mercer affair and Franklin's illness, the Roosevelts' marriage had emerged as a partnership of equals.

In 1924, Franklin had discovered Warm Springs— a small, run-down resort in Georgia's western hills. The warm mineral waters that flowed into the swimming pool there had reportedly helped other polio victims. Franklin believed that Warm Springs had healing potential. In 1926, he bought the facility and its surrounding 1,200 acres, financing the purchase with part of his inheritance. In 1927, he established the Georgia Warm Springs Foundation for Infantile Paralysis to help polio victims. Warm Springs with its soothing waters became Franklin's second home—replacing Campobello as his favorite retreat.

Eleanor, meanwhile, continued her own growth. As her inner strength blossomed, so did her interest in politics. Asked to define a "modern wife's job" by *Good Housekeeping* magazine, she replied that a woman must "develop her own interests, to carry on a stimulating life of her own..." Eleanor did so, nurturing the many friendships she had made among women like herself during her political travels.

After being stricken with polio, Franklin found the 88-degree waters of Warm Springs, Georgia, soothing. He eventually bought the former resort and established a foundation to assist others afflicted by the disease.

One afternoon in the late summer of 1924, Eleanor and her good friends Nancy Cook and Marion Dickerman were picnicking with Franklin along a small stream on the Roosevelt property in Hyde Park. All four agreed that they would miss outings such as these once the cold weather arrived. Franklin came up with the idea of building a cottage along the stream that the friends could

On a visit to Mount Vernon, George Washington's Virginia home, Eleanor poses with students and faculty from Todhunter School.

use as a year-round getaway. He gave the three women a lifetime lease on the property and hired an architect. Overseeing the cottage's construction during the following year was a welcome distraction for Franklin as he balanced family life with political ambition.

The first structure constructed on the site was a two-story Dutch colonial cottage made of fieldstone. Because Dutch settlers of the region had called the area "Val-Kill" (*val* means "waterfall" and *kill* means "stream"), and the cottage was early Dutch Colonial in design, Eleanor named the site Val-Kill. Cook and Dickerman would reside here for some twenty years, with Eleanor as a frequent visitor.

In 1926, a larger building was constructed nearby. In it, Val-Kill Industries was formed. The small factory the three women—Cook, Dickerman, and Roosevelt—operated produced furniture, and later, weavings and pewter goods. The factory stayed in business for ten years, sometimes employing as many as sixty craftsmen. Cook, a talented woodworker, oversaw the running of the operation.

Around the same time, Eleanor began teaching at Todhunter School, a private academy for girls located in Manhattan, where Marion Dickerman was an administrator. Eleanor greatly enjoyed teaching these young women and when Todhunter's founder decided to return to her home in England, Roosevelt, Dickerman, and Cook bought the school.

In the Spotlight

Keeping Franklin's long-term political goals in mind and enjoying her newfound sense of self-confidence, Eleanor continued to appear in the public eye. Eleanor gave her first radio broadcast in 1925, and in 1926, she vice-chaired the Women's City Club of New York's legislative committee. She also continued giving speeches and writing articles, such as "What I Want Most Out of Life" and "Women Must Learn to Play the Game as Men Do." In the latter article, published in April 1928, Eleanor offered advice to women who planned to enter politics. Also in 1928, in an attempt to keep up with her rapidly growing personal correspondence, Eleanor hired Malvina "Tommy" Thompson as her secretary—a position Thompson would hold until her death in 1953.

Writing later about his family life during these years, the Roosevelts' son Elliott commented that "Mother's year-round schedule of keeping busy meant that she had limited time for her

Val-Kill

After Val-Kill Industries closed in 1936, the factory building was renovated and became Eleanor's private retreat—Val-Kill Cottage. The "Big House" at Hyde Park had always been Sara's domain. Val-Kill was entirely Eleanor's. The rambling two-story, stucco structure included seven bedrooms, two large porches, two living rooms, and a dormitory for younger guests. Outside there was a swimming pool, tennis court, children's playhouse, and a large picnic area. Visitors over the years included friends, family, and the famous—among them President John F. Kennedy, Russian premier Nikita Khrushchev, and Indian prime minister Jawaharlal Nehru. Britain's prime minister, Winston Churchill, floated in the pool, cigar clamped firmly in his mouth. Ethiopian emperor Haile Selassie sat on the floor and watched television. The home's style was relaxed and comfortable. Photographs decorated the walls and tabletops. "Val-Kill," Eleanor said, "is something of my own."

After Franklin's death, the "Big House" was given by the family to the government as a historic site. Eleanor stayed on at Val-Kill until her death in 1962, when the property was inherited by her youngest son, John. In 1970, Val-Kill was sold to developers, who announced plans for a commercial project. Fearing Val-Kill's destruction, preservationists went into action. In 1977, legislation designated Val-Kill as the Eleanor Roosevelt National Historic Site, the only property in the United States honoring a first lady.

Stone Cottage, the first residence built at Val-Kill.

As Franklin struggled with post-polio rehabilitation efforts, Eleanor's frequent public appearances helped to keep the Roosevelt name in the news. This photo was taken during a visit to the Children's Museum of Brooklyn.

family." The children were away at various boarding schools during much of the year, seldom seeing their parents. Perhaps sensing the "separateness" of her family, Eleanor later wrote that she was sorry she had not been more involved in the upbringing of her three oldest children. She hoped to be more of a presence in the lives of her two youngest sons. Quite often, though, these efforts were hindered by her frequently critical mother-in-law. Unfortunately, Eleanor and Franklin's lives of independence came with a price—a lack of closeness and "connectedness" with their children.

After he was nominated as the Democratic candidate for governor of New York in 1928, Franklin immediately took to the campaign trail—in part to silence rumors about his health and physical limitations. Averaging half a dozen speeches a day, he traveled throughout the state by train and by car, often with Eleanor by his side. Listening to the same speech over and over could become boring. Sometimes humor was the only way to get through it. Louis Howe and others, wrote Eleanor, "would stand at the back of the hall when Franklin was making the same speech for the umpty-umpth time and make faces at me, trying to break up the apparent interest with which I was listening."

Attending a New York antique show in 1932, Eleanor sits at a reproduction desk produced by Val-Kill Industries.

Despite a nationwide Republican sweep, Democrat Franklin won the New York **gubernatorial** election—but by a slim margin. (Two years later, for his second term, he would win by a **landslide**.) Sworn in on January 1, 1929, Franklin stood in the same chamber where he had watched Theodore Roosevelt take the oath of office for governor exactly thirty years before. At this time, plans were already being set in motion for Franklin to continue further along in his famous relative's footsteps.

Eleanor did not look forward to the return to Albany as wife of the governor. She did not want to put aside all that she had accomplished and all that she had experienced. Instead, she divided her time between social duties in Albany, teaching in New York City, and a continued commitment to the issues of the day nationwide—particularly those that impacted women. The sight of the state's first lady dashing through the train station—as she juggled her many responsibilities—was not an uncommon one. It never occurred to Eleanor that, as the wife of the state's governor, she could ask that the train be held for her. Taking advantage of her special status was something Eleanor would not, *could* not, do. It was simply against her nature. She also refused to travel in an official limousine as she journeyed throughout New York. In fact, Eleanor often drove

Eleanor serves lunch to unemployed women and their children at a Depression-era soup kitchen. Some critics felt her activism was "unbecoming" for someone in Eleanor's position.

Poignant symbol of America's economic turmoil, a destitute man leans against a vacant storefront during the Great Depression. Franklin Roosevelt's New Deal legislation brought hope to many homeless and unemployed citizens.

herself as she took on the role not only of her husband's eyes and ears—but also of his *legs*. Limited by his paralysis, Franklin asked Eleanor to go where he could not. More and more, the people of New York noticed her attention to detail, her genuine concern for less fortunate people, and her awareness of the issues of the day. Eleanor's popularity soared with voters.

Ironically, her popularity did *not* soar with her children. James Roosevelt said of his mother, "She found it easier to give than to get, to do for than to have done for her. Mother loved all mankind, but she did not know how to let her children love her." And Eleanor's oldest child, her daughter, Anna, noted that, while Eleanor did her "duty" as a mother—making sure the children were well fed, properly clothed, and educated—"she had no real insight into the needs of a child for primary closeness to a parent." As a young mother, Eleanor had lacked the confidence to establish important bonds with her children. Years later she noted that, had she done a better job as a parent, perhaps her children "would have had far happier childhoods." (The impact may have been far-reaching as the five surviving Roosevelt children would go on to marry a total of nineteen times, more than half of these marriages ending in divorce.)

To the White House

Although 1929 appeared to start out as a year of prosperity, people's hopes crashed by October—along with the stock

During his 1932 presidential campaign, Franklin stops to shake hands with a Georgia farmer while on his way to Warm Springs.

Campaigning for the presidency, Franklin D. Roosevelt visits Indianapolis in the fall of 1932, while Americans everywhere battled the impact of the Great Depression.

market. By 1930, Franklin's second year as governor, four million Americans were out of work. The number would rise to six million during the following year, and double to twelve million by 1932. Although President Herbert Hoover continued to assure the American public that change was just around the corner, the hardships of the **Great Depression** had set in and the grim reality of life on the breadlines spoke differently. Change *was* just around the corner—but it was a change in the country's leadership and direction.

Franklin's campaign train, the "Roosevelt Special," pulls out of the Albany, New York, station on a campaign swing. Daughter Anna stands next to her father, while Eleanor is at far right.

At the Democratic National Convention held during the summer of 1932 in Chicago, Franklin Delano Roosevelt was named his party's candidate for president. "My husband," Eleanor wrote, "believed that he could meet the tremendous crisis the country was facing better than anyone else in the party."

Franklin set out on a grueling cross-country campaign schedule. Speaking from the rear platform of his railroad car, on a train dubbed "the Roosevelt Special," he spoke with confidence of the country's future. Although Eleanor knew this was what she and Louis Howe had worked for during the past decade, she would privately admit that, "I did not want my husband to be president…. It was pure selfishness on my part, and I never mentioned my feelings on the subject to him." Instead, Eleanor—and often one or more of their children—joined Franklin on the campaign trail. One reporter referred to Eleanor as Franklin's "devoted helpmate," never sensing the regret with which she looked at the possibility of becoming first lady.

Reluctance and Regret

To Eleanor, becoming first lady meant giving up nearly all the things that mattered most to her—her freedom, her memberships in various organizations, her teaching, her ability to contribute to her husband's political advancement, and most importantly, her ability to speak out. In prior administrations, the role of first lady was largely ceremonial. Presidential wives usually appeared as silent, smiling hostesses whose greatest energies were focused on beautification projects or social functions. Eleanor did not want to fade into the woodwork. However, she was keenly aware that it was *Franklin* the public had elected. Somehow she had to make the best of her new role.

"My husband believed that he could meet the tremendous crisis the country was facing better than anyone else in the party."

Among the reporters Eleanor met during the 1932 campaign was Lorena Hickok. Known as "Hick" to her friends, this pioneering journalist began her career as the society editor for a Milwaukee newspaper—a position she hated. After making a name for herself following a move to the city desk and stints at other publications, Hick became a feature writer for the Associated Press in 1928. She was highly respected by her

In 1932, Lorena Hickok was the highest paid female reporter employed by the Associated Press. Her encouragement led Eleanor to write the well-known column, "My Day."

predominantly male colleagues. Sensing a change in the country's political future, Hick requested the assignment of reporting on the Roosevelt campaign. In Hick, Eleanor sensed a kindred spirit. The two would become close friends.

On Election Day, Franklin won by a landslide. For Eleanor, the road ahead was not as clear. With this victory, it was apparent that the American public had looked beyond the wheelchair and the withered legs to give Franklin Roosevelt their full support. Now it was up to him to lead the country out from the depths of the Great Depression into a future filled with promise.

CHAPTER 7

The President's Wife

As I saw it, this meant the end of any personal life of my own.

In 1933, Eleanor Roosevelt assumed her new role as first lady somewhat reluctantly, partly because she had to give up so much. Franklin had asked her to stop teaching at the Todhunter School and to resign from positions she held in various organizations, including the League of Women Voters, the Democratic National Committee, and the Women's Trade Union League. Eleanor announced that, once in the White House, she would be just "plain, ordinary Mrs. Roosevelt."

But only two days after her husband's inauguration, Eleanor—acting on the suggestion of her friend Lorena Hickok—met with thirty-five women journalists, announcing that she would begin holding regular press conferences. No other first lady had ever done this. Although the president's advisers worried that Eleanor might cause problems for the administration, Franklin did not. Just the fact that a first lady would speak regularly to the press was news in itself, but these press conferences would be open only to *female* reporters.

This announcement had a big impact on the field of journalism and created many new opportunities for women. Before this, most news jobs were held by men. This was just the first of many such actions that Eleanor

Eleanor established the precedent of scheduling weekly press conferences limited to women reporters only. Beginning on March 6, 1933, she held 348 conferences during the Roosevelt Administration.

would undertake as she shaped her role as first lady into something quite different than it had ever been before.

At her press conferences Eleanor often brought up topics that were controversial in an attempt to make sure people talked about certain issues. As she began to speak out more and more, critics sometimes called her "Empress Eleanor" or "Madam President." By the time her husband became president, Eleanor had also developed a thicker skin that would serve her well in the years ahead. The timid young woman who lacked self-confidence was gone. It was not easy, but Eleanor had found the courage to stand up for herself and for what she believed in—and that courage helped her become the most outspoken and active first lady in history.

Eleanor Airborne

When Franklin Roosevelt became president in 1933, many Americans still considered flying a risky way to travel. However, the "Flying First Lady" did not agree. She logged more hours in the air during the 1930s than any other female passenger and also became one of the first women to fly at night.

Eleanor had great admiration for female pilots and supported the expanding role of women in aviation. One evening in 1933, the pilot Amelia Earhart and her husband, G. P. Putnam, were overnight guests at the White House. Dressed in formal gowns and white gloves after an evening function, Amelia and Eleanor took off for a flight from Washington to Baltimore and back. When reporters asked how it felt to be piloted by a woman, Eleanor replied, "I'd give a lot to do it myself!" In fact, Amelia did give the first lady some basic introductory lessons. In addition to supporting women as pilots and the aviation industry in general, Eleanor also endorsed African American pilots. On a visit to the aeronautical school begun at Alabama's Tuskegee Institute during World War II, Eleanor asked to fly with one of the aviators there. Her flight—and the publicity that followed—brought crucial support to the school's aviation training program and lent support to the African American male pilots in the war effort.

Amelia Earhart in the cockpit of her plane after setting a new altitude record for women.

Syndicated Columnist

Not long after moving into the White House, Eleanor also began to write a monthly column for a popular magazine, *Woman's Home Companion*, donating the fee she was paid to charity. Eleanor entitled her column "I Want You to Write to Me," and readers responded with enthusiasm. In 1933 alone, she received more than 300,000 letters—requests for money, housing, food, clothing, and advice, as well as criticisms and compliments. Although she could not respond personally to every letter, she made certain each one received an answer of some kind.

Usually, Eleanor dictated the material to her secretary, Malvina Thompson, while traveling, knitting, or finishing a meal. But sometimes—often late at night—she simply typed them herself.

In 1933 alone, she received more than 300,000 letters—requests for money, housing, food, clothing, and advice, as well as criticisms and compliments.

Despite her busy schedule, Eleanor Roosevelt always took the time to write letters to her good friend Lorena Hickok. These letters were usually filled with details about life in the White House, accounts of her travels, and the general events of Eleanor's day. "Hick" felt these letters would make an interesting column . . . and so an idea was born.

Two years later, Eleanor began writing a column called "My Day." "My Day" not only mentioned the famous guests who visited the White House, but also the "regular folk" whom Eleanor met in her travels. Some columns contained stories or anecdotes she wished to share, others provided suggestions about daily life

MY DAY— By Eleanor Roosevelt

HYDE PARK, N. Y., Nov. 6.— Yesterday afternoon went quietly on its way. Some of us took a walk and returned to the big house for tea, where we found Johnny and Anne and their little dachshund, "Percy," had arrived from Boston.

I think what I enjoy most about these historic occasions is that they bring together what family there is within reach, and we sometimes hear by telephone, at least, the voices of the rest of the family. Quite a large group came to a picnic supper at the cottage, but by 9 o'clock we were back at the big house. We sat around radios in the dif-

MRS. ROOSEVELT

Anna, and afterwards with Jan and Elliott.

Anna told me that our eld grandchildren had been so c cerned that they had decide prepare them in case of de but the children looked so jected that nobody was happy til they heard that the ver was victory.

To children, of course, i just a case of winning a c paign. To the rest of us, I th it is rather terrifying for a g unlimited power known you by a ple of a great nation is so thing to make men proud grateful, but at the same tim is a heavy responsibility.

The returns seem to indic a vote of real confidence, wl must mean that the people the nation approve of the dot tic policies as well as the cou charted in our foreign relatic

It was a vigorous fight now that it is over, for the s of the country as a whole, let hope that those who have had accept a verdict with which t did not agree, will help in ev way to carry out the will of people, having faith in the g

("…one should always sleep in all of one's guest beds, to make sure that they are comfortable"). Some discussed marriage or raising children. There were candid insights into the first lady's life, as well as observations about political issues of the day ("…without equality there can be no democracy"). Topics ranged from **literacy** to women's rights, from the convenience of frozen vegetables to details about Eleanor's garden. Six days a week, "My Day" was read by millions of Americans who enjoyed Eleanor's friendly, easy-to-read writing style—almost as though she were corresponding with a good friend.

As the wife of a head of state, Eleanor also had certain social responsibilities. The White House during the Roosevelt presidency was, one historian wrote, like "a small, private hotel." Friends, family, and foreign dignitaries came and went on a regular basis. Key Roosevelt administration officials sometimes *lived* in the White House for months on end. These residents at one time or another included Louis Howe, Lorena Hickok, Malvina Thompson, and the president's secretary, Missy LeHand, as well as various Roosevelt children and grandchildren. During 1939, Eleanor noted: "4,729 people came to a lunch, dinner, or tea; 323 people were house guests; and 23,267 were officially received at receptions."

During the first months of his presidency, Franklin Roosevelt set about providing a "New Deal" for American citizens who had been hit hard by the Great Depression. A series of programs and agencies such as the National Recovery Administration, the Federal Emergency Relief Administration, and the Works Progress Administration, were set up to provide relief for those affected by the economic situation. Sensing the need for an agency that would primarily benefit young Americans, Eleanor helped convince her husband to form the National Youth Administration. This agency provided job training to young men and women, as well as financial assistance to students.

"My Day"

Eleanor submitted her first "My Day" column for publication on December 30, 1935. Although she initially signed a contract for only five years, these daily reports became so popular that Eleanor continued to write them until 1962. The last was published just weeks before she died. The only time the columns were interrupted was during a four-day period in 1945 right after Franklin's death. In its first year, "My Day" appeared in twenty newspapers. By year's end, that figure had nearly tripled and eventually rose to 135.

In addition to more than 8,000 columns, Eleanor Roosevelt also produced twenty-seven books and more than 550 articles. On average, she gave seventy-five speeches a year—all of which she composed herself. After she left the White House, she still received an average of 21,000 pieces of mail a year. Many letters were written in response to items that appeared in Eleanor's popular columns.

A frequent visitor to the Roosevelt White House, Eleanor's daughter, Anna, poses with her son, John, and his smiling grandmother.

On the Road

As she had in New York when her husband was governor, Eleanor now traveled throughout the country and reported to Franklin about how Americans were faring. During the administration's first year, she traveled more than 40,000 miles. She visited the tar-paper shacks of sharecroppers, square-danced in high school gymnasiums, and descended deep into coal mines. Whenever possible, Eleanor preferred to travel simply and without fanfare. She also refused Secret Service protection, trusting that the American people would do her no harm. The majority of the public Eleanor met appreciated the first lady's sympathetic nature, boundless energy, and genuine concern. By Franklin's second term as president, Eleanor's popularity among voters equaled—and sometimes exceeded—that of her husband. For Franklin—restricted by both the pressures of the presidency and his paralysis—Eleanor's input on issues of the day and her reports from her travels were essential.

Most of the time, Eleanor and Franklin would sit down to talk right after she returned—often over lunch or dinner. What had she seen? Who had she spoken to? What were the conditions like? What did people tell her? Were the government's programs working? The more she traveled for her husband, the more Eleanor learned what to look for and where to look for it. If their busy schedules did not allow Eleanor and Franklin time to meet, Eleanor would send a memo to her husband summarizing all that she had learned. Eventually an "Eleanor basket" was placed in Franklin's room where the memos were deposited—sometimes in great numbers. At one point, Franklin reportedly said to his wife, "Eleanor, three

Wearing a miner's cap, the well-traveled first lady makes the first of several highly publicized descents into coal mines to view working conditions there.

In 1936, diners at New York's Paradise Restaurant merrily celebrate Roosevelt's landslide second-term victory. Carrying 46 states and 61 percent of the popular vote, the election results were unprecedented in modern times.

memos a night—not 12, not 20, not 30. I will initial them and deal with them by morning."

With the entry of the United States into World War II in 1941, Eleanor Roosevelt's role as first lady changed yet again. Although she did not abandon domestic issues, she now focused on international concerns such as the status of **refugees** fleeing Nazi Germany, Allied troop morale around the globe, and women's roles in the defense industry. All four Roosevelt sons served in the military, and each was decorated for bravery. Eleanor—like mothers around the world—suffered the constant worry that she might not see them again.

During a visit to England in 1942, she saw the damage that German bombs had done and the tremendous contribution British women were making to the war effort through their work in factories. The following year, she traveled 23,000 miles to Australia, New Zealand, and seventeen Pacific islands to visit hundreds of thousands of soldiers. Dressed simply in a Red Cross uniform and wearing comfortable shoes, Eleanor bent over the beds of wounded soldiers, offering a touch, a smile, and some words of comfort. Many times it was hard for her to keep tears from flowing. When told that the president's wife would be visiting troops overseas, Admiral William Halsey had initially branded her a do-gooder who would only be an inconvenience for his men. However, after seeing the first lady in action, Halsey could only praise her efforts—and her fortitude. By the time she returned to Washington after her five-week journey, she had lost thirty pounds.

In addition to the challenges of social reform and a world at war, the years in Washington brought sadness to Eleanor and

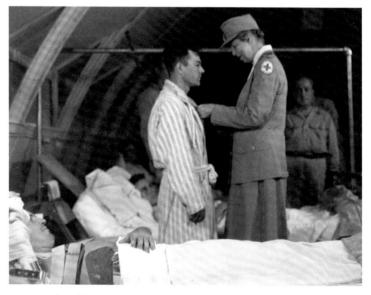

During one leg of her lengthy trip to the southwestern Pacific, Eleanor awards a medal to a soldier whose ship, the USS *Navajo*, was torpedoed and sunk in 1943.

Franklin. Shortly before beginning his second term as president in 1936, Franklin lost his trusted friend and adviser of a quarter century, Louis Howe. The year 1941 was perhaps the worst—that summer, Franklin's long-time secretary and confidant, Missy LeHand, suffered a series of strokes and would die three years later. Two weeks shy of her eighty-seventh birthday, Sara Roosevelt died on September 7, 1941. Franklin, her devoted only child, was by her side at the end.

In addition to the challenges, the years in Washington brought sadness to Eleanor and Franklin.

For Franklin, the loss was enormous. For Eleanor there was a grudging respect for her mother-in-law—but nothing more. "It is dreadful," wrote Eleanor to her daughter, Anna, "to have lived so close to someone for 36 years & feel no deep affection or sense of loss." During her transformation from shy and insecure young bride to outspoken first lady and reformer, Eleanor had suffered too many hurts and disappointments in her relationship with the strong-willed Sara.

Less than three weeks after the death of Franklin's mother, Eleanor lost her fifty-one-year-old brother, Hall. Six years older than he was, Eleanor had acted as a surrogate mother to Hall—settling him at school, keeping a room for his visits, offering love and encouragement throughout his life. But just like their father, Hall struggled with alcoholism and never recovered. It was a sad time for both Eleanor and Franklin.

Despite the daily challenges Eleanor faced during her life in the White House, perhaps more than anything else, being first lady gave her an established national—and international—platform from which she could speak out on issues that needed to be addressed. Most of these issues were controversial, but they affected the

After landing in Australia, Eleanor stands with Lt. General Harmon (left) and Admiral Halsey (right) in front of the plane in which she logged countless miles visiting troops and helping to raise wartime morale.

country, and ultimately, the world. Much later in her life, Eleanor would write that, "It was not until I reached middle years that I had the courage to develop interests of my own." The seeds of Eleanor's social conscience had been planted years before when she volunteered in New York City **settlement houses**. Now, as the wife of the president, Eleanor was able to turn the position of first lady from a role that was mainly ornamental to one of activism. It was an accomplishment she relished.

The Outdoorswoman

An appreciation for athletic competition and a love of the outdoors are not the traits one usually considers when thinking about Eleanor Roosevelt, yet both were important parts of her personality. One of the proudest days of her life, Eleanor once wrote, was when she made the varsity field hockey team at Allenswood Academy.

Prior to his illness, Franklin had devoted most of his family time to the children's athletic endeavors. When polio struck in the summer of 1921, Franklin Jr. was only seven, and John just five. Eleanor wrote, "I had two young boys who had to learn to do the things that boys must do—swim, ride and camp. . . . I had no confidence in my ability to do physical things at this time. . . . It began to dawn upon me that if these two youngest boys were going to have a normal existence without a father to do these things with them, I would have to become a good deal more companionable and more of an all-round person than I had ever been before." And she did.

Eleanor, armed and dangerous, aims for a target at Chazy Lake in the Adirondacks, 1934.

CHAPTER 8

Taking a Stand

Do what you feel in your heart to be right—
for you'll be criticized anyway.
You'll be damned if you do,
and damned if you don't.

As first lady, Eleanor championed many causes. Among these were housing reform, child welfare, world peace, and unemployment. However, it was to civil rights that Eleanor turned her strongest focus—taking an often unpopular stand on this very controversial issue. For the rest of her life, the rights of humankind would remain at the heart of her activism.

NEGROES
ARE BARRED
From Theatres
in the
Nation's Capital

Exiting her car outside a Washington, D.C., theater in 1940, Eleanor encounters a picket line protesting local discriminatory practices.

When Franklin Roosevelt was inaugurated president in 1933, **racial discrimination** was commonly practiced throughout the United States—particularly in the southern states. African Americans were not allowed in many hotels, theaters, restaurants, and other public facilities. In some areas, they were not even permitted to vote. Eleanor Roosevelt felt that this denial of basic rights to a large portion of American citizens should not be tolerated. She was not afraid to act on her beliefs and often spoke out or wrote articles outlining her stand on this issue.

Roy Wilkins, a former director of the National Association for the Advancement of Colored People (NAACP), noted, "Mrs. Roosevelt was the Negro's true friend." But many white people were extremely displeased by Eleanor Roosevelt's stand on civil rights, and she was often sharply criticized in the press. One woman, responding to a column of Eleanor's that covered civil rights, even wrote, "I don't mean to be rude, but do you have colored blood in your family, as you seem to derive so much pleasure from associating with colored folks?" In later years, when she was in her seventies, Eleanor even received a death threat from the Ku Klux Klan, a southern white **extremist** group.

For the rest of her life, the rights of humankind would remain at the heart of her activism.

Franklin Roosevelt, on the other hand, was much more conservative and more hesitant to address this issue as directly as his wife. Strong statements by the president in support of civil rights might anger the many powerful members of Congress who came from the South. Their support of New Deal programs, and later, the war effort, was essential.

In the Public Eye

In 1927, Eleanor had met Mary McLeod Bethune, a politically prominent African American. The two became close friends as well as political allies. Mary Bethune later founded the National Organization of Colored Women, a group working to end discrimination and **segregation**. In 1936, with Eleanor's support, Mary Bethune became director of Negro Affairs for the National Youth Administration in which she was able to actively lobby for issues affecting African Americans.

Standing beside her friend and colleague Mary McLeod Bethune, director of the National Youth Administration, Eleanor speaks to attendees of the 1939 National Negro Youth Conference in Washington, D.C.

Barred from performing at Constitution Hall because of her skin color, the famous contralto Marian Anderson sings to a crowd of more than 75,000 from the steps of the Lincoln Memorial on Easter Sunday, 1939.

In 1938, Eleanor Roosevelt and Mary Bethune attended the Southern Conference for Human Welfare in Birmingham, Alabama. This meeting was held to address the socio-economic concerns of *all* people living in the South—black and white. Upon arrival Eleanor was told by police officers that she could not sit with her friend because city segregation laws would not permit it. Rather than move to the area for "Whites Only," Eleanor placed her chair in the aisle directly between the two sections of the auditorium—her action made a definite statement of protest.

The following year, Eleanor learned that the highly talented opera singer Marian Anderson had been barred by the Daughters of the American Revolution (DAR) from performing at their Constitution Hall facility because she was an African American. In protest, Eleanor resigned from the organization—announcing this decision in her widely read column "My Day." She also wrote a letter to the DAR saying, "…I am in complete disagreement with the attitude taken in refusing Constitution Hall to a great artist. You have set an example which seems to me unfortunate, and I feel obliged to send in to you my resignation. You had an opportunity to lead in an enlightened way and it seems to me that your organization has failed." Arrangements were then made by the Roosevelt administration for Anderson to perform at the Lincoln Memorial where she appeared before an estimated audience of more than 75,000. The concert also was broadcast to millions of listeners. Once again, through her actions, Eleanor had made her feelings about racial discrimination clearly known.

A Woman's Place

Equal opportunities for women presented another area of focus in Eleanor's commitment to individual rights. When, shortly after her husband took office, the first lady announced that her press conferences would be restricted to female journalists only, many newspapers were forced to hire their first female reporters. Within the Roosevelt administration, Eleanor encouraged her husband to bring in qualified women and did

February 26, 1939.

My dear Mrs. ~~Robert:~~ Henry M. Jr.

I am afraid that I have never been a very
~~useful member of the Daughters of the~~
~~American Revolution, so I know it will~~
~~make very little difference to you whether~~
I resign, or whether I continue to be a
member of your organization.

However, I am in complete disagreement
with the attitude taken in refusing
Constitution Hall to a great artist.
You have set an example which seems to
me unfortunate, and I feel obliged to
send in to you my resignation.   You
had an opportunity to lead in an enlightened way and it seems to me that your
organization has failed.

I realize that many people will not agree
with me, but feeling as I do this seems
to me the only proper procedure to
follow.

            Very sincerely yours,

Eleanor's letter of resignation from the DAR was submitted after that organization's refusal to let Marian Anderson perform at Constitution Hall. Press coverage of the first lady's very public stand helped to focus national attention on civil rights issues.

not hesitate to suggest specific individuals. By the end of Franklin's first term in office, more women held government positions than ever before. The Roosevelt administration also was the first in history to have a woman appointed to a cabinet post. Frances Perkins, who had been Franklin's state industrial commissioner when he was governor of New York, continued to Washington and served as Roosevelt's secretary of labor in each of his four terms of office.

During the New Deal era, Eleanor supported the idea of a female counterpart to the all-male Civilian Conservation Corps (CCC)—a government agency that offered unemployed young men jobs in national conservation programs. She envisioned residential camps where unemployed women between the ages of eighteen and twenty-five could participate in a structured program of mostly outdoor activities that were educationally and environmentally oriented. Dubbed the "She She She Camps" by critics, they did not enjoy the tremendous success of the CCC. However, 8,500 women did benefit from participation in the program.

Just as Eleanor Roosevelt changed the role of first lady into something it had never been before, so did World War II have an impact on the role of women. Fewer men were available to join the home-front workforce because they were serving in the military, so more and more women took up the slack. Between the years 1940 and 1944, the number of women in war-related jobs rose 460 percent. When wartime manufacturing and production were at their peak, almost twenty million women were employed—nearly one-third of the nonmilitary workforce. Advising young women not to succumb to wartime pressure and marry too hastily, Eleanor noted that, "If I were of debutante age,

Appointed secretary of labor in the Roosevelt Administration, Frances Perkins served as the nation's first female cabinet member. Here she surveys work on San Francisco's Golden Gate project in 1935.

Eleanor addresses residents at a camp for unemployed young women at Bear Mountain, New York. By 1936, ninety such camps provided training and unemployment relief for some 5,000 women annually.

I would go into a factory, where I could learn a skill and be useful." Her support of women working for the war effort led to the first government funds ever spent for the construction of day-care facilities. Here again, Franklin did not try to change or restrict his wife's behavior when it came to the support of women in the workplace. Instead, he let Eleanor take the spotlight and thereby defused possible criticism of his administration.

In an article titled "American Women in the War" written in 1944, Eleanor praised not only the women working in factories and production lines at home, but also the women in the armed forces who tirelessly supported the troops. "Our women are serving actively in many ways in this war," she wrote, "and they are doing a grand job on both the fighting front and the home front." She cited examples of the dedication of the 12,000 or so army and navy nurses who were stationed overseas, as well as the many women serving in civilian hospitals at home. Eleanor also supported the idea of women as military pilots, calling them "a weapon waiting to be used."

Taking a stand on issues she felt were of the utmost importance to society was a key component of Eleanor's personality. However, taking a stand often meant facing public criticism. The shyly hesitant young woman who had married Franklin Roosevelt in 1905 could never have withstood the relentless barrage of public comment that Eleanor faced nearly every day as first lady. In 1944, she wrote an article titled "How to

On a wartime goodwill tour of Great Britain, Eleanor visited women factory workers and surveyed German bomb damage to London neighborhoods.

American women joined the wartime work force by the thousands. "Women," said Eleanor, "will be given a chance to expand their horizons." This former Texas sales-clerk made the switch to aircraft maintenance.

Take Criticism." In it, she cautioned against letting criticism dictate behavior. Focusing on negative comments and nothing else would, she believed, make life unbearable. "Everyone must live their own life in their own way," she wrote, "and not according to anybody else's idea." Through her activism, Eleanor Roosevelt became a **spokesperson** for many who had not had a voice before, and— despite the risk of personal criticism—did not hesitate to bring controversial issues to the public's attention again and again.

No Ordinary Time

On July 18, 1940, Eleanor Roosevelt became the first presidential wife to address a national political convention. Franklin's bid for an unprecedented third term, combined with his controversial choice of a running mate—Secretary of Agriculture Henry Wallace—had created chaos among the Democratic delegates.

Despite her own reservations about spending another four years in the White House, Eleanor flew to Chicago at her husband's request. Her speech, given primarily from notes and not a pre-written text, spoke to the heart: "We people in the United States have got to realize today that we face a grave and serious situation. . . . We cannot tell from day to day what may come. This is no ordinary time. No time for weighing anything except what we can do best for the country as a whole, and that responsibility rests on each and every one of us as individuals. No man who is a candidate or who is President can carry this situation alone. This is only carried by a united people who love their country and who will live for it . . . to the fullest of their ability."

The response was overwhelming. Wild cheering and applause greeted Eleanor's speech and the party united to nominate Wallace as vice President.

Eleanor addresses the 1940 Democratic National Convention in Chicago.

CHAPTER 9

The Last Term

You have to accept whatever comes and the only important thing is that you meet it with the best you have to give.

Prior to the election of Franklin Roosevelt, no U.S. president had ever served more than two terms in office. As he guided the country through the financial challenges of the Great Depression and then steered a steady course during World War II, Franklin Roosevelt was viewed by many citizens as a father figure, a savior, a friend, and a fearless leader. Facing a fourth term as president, his steady voice was as familiar as that of a family member. Especially to the nation's youth, he seemed invincible—the man who had *always* led the country.

In 1933, Franklin Roosevelt had entered the White House full of vitality, eager to face the challenges that lay ahead. However, by 1944, the strain of serving as president for more than a decade had begun to take its toll. Those who hadn't seen him for several months were shocked by the changes in Franklin's appearance. He had lost weight; his face sagged; his hands trembled; and he had a soft cough that wouldn't go away.

At first, doctors thought Franklin was still recovering from a case of the flu. Further tests revealed that his symptoms were actually those of congestive heart failure. Better eating habits, less smoking, more rest, and medication were all prescribed. Franklin's condition began to improve noticeably. However, worries about the president's health continued—not only among his family but also among those who hoped he would serve a fourth term. Eleanor, deeply committed to social issues both nationally and internationally, was torn between concern for her husband and concern for her country's future. She may have somehow sensed that time was running out.

With the country still at war, for Franklin the choice was clear. "I have as little right to withdraw as the soldier has to leave his post in the line." At the Democratic National Convention in July, he was nominated once again for president, with Harry S Truman as his vice-presidential candidate. When the votes were counted in November, Franklin Roosevelt had been re-elected to

Missouri-native Harry S Truman signed on as Franklin's running mate in 1944 not knowing he would take over the duties of the presidency less than a year later.

The FIRST Lady

Eleanor Roosevelt was born during the final years of the Victorian era, at a time when the behavior of women was severely restricted. Yet throughout her life, she supported the rights of women. She strongly believed in women's abilities and was quick to promote their accomplishments. "I have a firm belief in the ability and power of women to achieve the things they want to achieve," she wrote in a 1941 magazine article. Eleanor Roosevelt's own achievements were many. As first lady, Eleanor Roosevelt was the first wife of a president to

- Hold press conferences (and to admit only female reporters)
- Drive her own car
- Receive a presidential appointment (as assistant director of the Office of Civilian Defense, 1941–1942)
- Testify before a congressional committee
- Speak before a national party convention
- Travel by air
- Write a syndicated column
- Earn an income (which she donated to charity)
- Speak on the radio as a commentator

She was also the first *former* first lady to serve as a delegate to the United Nations.

For Franklin, Eleanor's outspokenness was often invaluable. Through her he was able to "test the waters" on controversial issues. If something Eleanor said was met with criticism, he might say, "I can't do anything about her." Meanwhile, Franklin was getting a real sense of just how far his administration could go in pushing for social change.

serve an unprecedented fourth term. However, this term would definitely be the last.

As early as 1938, Franklin had been thinking ahead to retirement and making plans.

That year, at a hilltop site on his family's Hyde Park property, he constructed his own retreat—Top Cottage. Like Eleanor's Val-Kill home, the structure was built in the Dutch architectural style commonly found throughout the Hudson Valley. This simple, informal home was a place where he planned to rest and relax and write his memoirs. Made primarily of fieldstone, Top Cottage was one of the first barrier-free buildings constructed in the United States that was fully accessible to a disabled person. In addition to family members, visitors had already included

Franklin and Eleanor pose with their 13 grandchildren at the White House on Inauguration Day, January 20, 1945.

Winston Churchill and King George VI of England. However, for now, retirement life at Top Cottage would have to wait until Franklin finished his final term as president.

The End of an Era

On Inauguration Day—January 20, 1945—the usual celebrations and large parades were not held because the country was still at war. Speaking from the south porch of the White House rather than the Capitol steps, Franklin kept his remarks brief. It took less than five minutes for him to deliver his speech. The weather was cold, the ceremony short. The nation's commander in chief got back to business, leaving just three days later for an important overseas conference in Yalta, Crimea (now Ukraine), with the British prime minister, Winston Churchill, and Joseph Stalin, Russia's leader.

One of Franklin Roosevelt's hopes at the Yalta Conference had been to lay a foundation for lasting peace after the war was over. Although the success of the conference was mixed, in that respect he was successful, as an agreement was reached to establish a new organization— the United Nations—for just that purpose.

Franklin—holding his Scottish terrier, Fala—visits with the caretaker's grandchild at Top Cottage. This 1941 photo is one of only two in existence showing the president in a wheelchair.

Reporting on the Yalta Conference to a joint session of Congress on March 1, the president shocked participants by appearing in his wheelchair. It was the first time he had ever done this. So carefully arranged were all of Franklin Roosevelt's public appearances that many people did not even realize he was completely paralyzed from the waist down.

Those attending the joint session were also surprised when Franklin did not stand to deliver his speech. Instead, he sat at a table below the podium. Before starting on the major portion of his remarks, he spoke very candidly saying, "I hope that you will pardon me for the unusual posture of sitting down during the presentation of what I want to say, but I know that you will realize it makes it a lot easier for me in not having to carry about ten pounds of steel around on the bottom of my legs." Clearly, the president was tired.

So carefully arranged were all of Franklin Roosevelt's public appearances that many people did not even realize he was paralyzed.

On March 29, Franklin Roosevelt left Washington for two weeks of rest at his small cottage in Warm Springs, Georgia. It was the last trip he would take as president. On April 12, while sitting at his desk working on some papers as an artist painted a portrait of him, he was struck by a massive cerebral hemorrhage and died later that day. Eleanor, told of the news in Washington, cabled her sons—all overseas on active duty—FATHER [SLIPPED] AWAY THIS AFTERNOON. HE DID HIS JOB TO THE END AS HE WOULD WANT [YOU] TO DO. Harry Truman answered an urgent call to come to the White House immediately. Eleanor broke the news of the president's death to him. Clearly stunned, it was a while

Just days after his fourth—and final—inauguration, a clearly exhausted Franklin attended the historic Yalta Conference with British Prime Minister Winston Churchill (left) and Soviet Premier Joseph Stalin (right).

before the vice president spoke. "Is there anything I can do for you?" he asked. Eleanor replied, "Is there anything *we* can do for *you*? For you are the one in trouble now."

Strength in Adversity

The reaction around the world was swift—and stunning. Soldiers in the field, hearing the news, wept openly. Franklin's death came on the eve of triumph. How could the president, whose firm hand had guided the country through the years of conflict, not be there to see the nation through to victory?

Less than a month after Franklin's death, the Nazi regime crumbled, and three months later, on August 14, Japan, too, surrendered.

A woman is supported by fellow mourners as the Roosevelt funeral procession travels through the nation's capital. Millions grieved worldwide at the news of Franklin's death.

"I felt as if I'd been struck a physical blow," wrote Winston Churchill, a strong ally and trusted friend. In a rare show of respect for another world leader, Stalin allowed Franklin Roosevelt's picture to appear on the front pages of Russian newspapers.

Staying at the Capitol only for Truman's brief swearing-in ceremony, Eleanor flew to Georgia, arriving in Warm Springs shortly before midnight. While her husband's death was a great loss, Eleanor received another crushing blow after she had arrived at the little cottage. Although Eleanor knew that two of Franklin's cousins had been with him when he died, she found out that someone else had been there as well—a Mrs. Rutherford. A few questions revealed the shattering news: Mrs. Rutherford was *Lucy Mercer* Rutherford, a recent widow. Unbeknownst to Eleanor, Lucy and Franklin had renewed their friendship, meeting a dozen or more times over the past few months. For

Holding a newspaper tribute to the fallen president, three children wait with
thousands of grief-stricken Americans for the Roosevelt funeral procession to pass
by along Washington's Constitution Avenue.

Eleanor, this news must have felt like a final betrayal; yet outwardly she gave no sign of the hurt she surely felt inside.

Traveling northward the next day on the same train that carried her husband's flag-draped coffin, Eleanor kept her window shade up most of the time so she could see the faces of the crowds—black, white, young, old—thousands, all grieving. For many Americans, Franklin Roosevelt was the only president they had ever known. Newspapers across the nation carried the somber headlines: "EXTRA! Roosevelt Dead. Cerebral Hemorrhage Proves Fatal; President Truman Sworn in Office." "Roosevelt Death Is Shock to the World." "Tears, Hysterics Greet FDR News in Capital." Already a flood of letters and telegrams expressing the grief of the nation and the world was pouring into the White House.

As night came all the train's lights were dimmed, except those in the car carrying the president's coffin. Past farms, towns, fields, and crossroads, the train continued on its twenty-three-hour journey northward to Washington's Union Station. There, Anna and Elliott joined their mother, and the president's casket was loaded onto a horse-drawn caisson (a two-wheeled military vehicle) that slowly traveled to the White House. Along the route were thousands of people—mostly silent, except for weeping, some kneeling along the sidewalks in prayer. Later that afternoon, a simple funeral service was held in the East Room. "It seemed to me that everyone in the world was there," Eleanor later wrote, "except three of my own sons." (Elliott, stationed at an air base in England, was able to make it back in time for the

Past farms, towns, fields, and crossroads, the train continued on its twenty-three-hour journey.

Entering the rose garden at Hyde Park, the president's flag-draped coffin passes between rows of soldiers standing at attention.

service. But John and Franklin Jr., serving at sea in the Pacific, and James, stationed in the Philippines, could not.) On her black dress, she wore only one simple piece of jewelry—the pin that Franklin had given her as a wedding gift forty years before.

Later that night Eleanor boarded the train once again as Franklin Roosevelt began his last journey—back to his beloved

Hyde Park. Also accompanying him in the train's seventeen cars were two of his children and their families, many friends and political allies, cabinet members, Supreme Court justices, the new president, eighteen reporters, and Franklin's little dog, Fala.

The next morning, under beautiful blue skies with the fragrance of spring in the air, the president's body was laid to rest in his mother's rose garden, behind the family home. After the graveside service, Eleanor remained behind for a few moments, then accepted President Truman's offer to ride back on the train to Washington. After twelve years in the White House, there was a tremendous amount to be done, and Eleanor felt she should turn the house over to its new occupants as soon as possible. By week's end, a thousand boxes had been packed and loaded onto twenty trucks.

Eleanor and Fala, the well-known Scottish terrier. Fala lived until 1952, and was buried at his master's feet in the Rose Garden at Hyde Park.

Eleanor stands with French General Charles de Gaulle (third from left) as he pays his respects at the Roosevelt gravesite in August 1945.

On her last day in the White House, Eleanor hosted a tea for the female reporters who had covered her years as first lady. Then, after spending her final night in the president's quarters, Eleanor said good-bye to the staff and boarded a train for New York City where she had a small apartment. Arriving at her front door, she was asked by a reporter for a statement. "The story is over," she said wearily. But she was wrong. Her story was not over—in some ways, *her* story was just beginning.

CHAPTER 10

First Lady of the World

It isn't enough to talk about peace.
One must believe in it.
And it isn't enough to believe in it.
One must work at it.

With the death of Franklin Roosevelt on April 12, 1945—at the beginning of his fourth term as president—Eleanor Roosevelt imagined that the remaining years of her life would be spent quietly. The months following Franklin's death were difficult. While Eleanor did not miss the "fish bowl" existence of life in the White House, she missed her husband...and her president. In August, when the war was at last truly over, Eleanor wrote to her daughter, Anna, "I miss Pa's voice, and the words he would have spoken."

Now sixty years old, Eleanor planned to divide her time between Val-Kill and a small apartment in New York City. After

Addressing the topic "The World We Live In—The World We Want," Eleanor speaks to those attending the International Assembly of Women in South Kortright, New York.

all, she reasoned, it had been her husband who people wanted to see, not the first lady. She could not have been more wrong. In the months to come, Eleanor would begin to move out from the shadow of her husband—and of the presidency. For the first time, she would truly begin to stand alone.

Although Franklin had given his Hyde Park home and thirty-three acres to the U.S. government to be designated as a historic site, he had arranged that his wife and children could still live there for the rest of their lives. However, all of the family members agreed that the estate was much too large to maintain, and that it made more sense to turn it over as soon as possible. After several months of dealing with the enormous task of sorting,

"I miss Pa's voice, and the words he would have spoken."

packing, distributing, and dividing up the huge number of personal belongings, the family signed over the estate in November of 1945. For herself, Eleanor took very little. As the president's widow, she was entitled to a number of benefits, but she politely turned down all but one of them—including her husband's pension. The only benefit she kept was the right to simply use her signature, instead of stamps, when mailing letters.

In the months after Franklin's death, Eleanor had been approached by a number of individuals about the possibility of running for political office or managing various political organizations—the positions of senator, governor, and even vice president, had all been mentioned. She was also asked to continue her "My Day" column, and to give a number of speeches and lectures. Although she was still trying to decide what her plans were for the future, Eleanor was certain that running for political office was not among them. In order to

In January 1946, Eleanor addressed fellow delegates from more than 50 countries at the first meeting of the United Nations General Assembly.

make her feelings known, she eventually wrote an article in 1946 for *Look* magazine, "Why I Do Not Choose to Run." By the time the article was published, Eleanor had already decided what she would be doing. President Truman had asked for her help with the new United Nations.

One Among Many

It had been Franklin Roosevelt who came up with the name "United Nations" to describe the member countries that would make up a permanent international organization for world peace following World War II. The UN was formally established on October 24, 1945—six months after Franklin's death. Returning to public service once again, in December 1945, Eleanor became a member of the first American delegation to the UN General Assembly. At first she had been hesitant to accept President Truman's appointment. After all, she was not a scholar, and she did not have experience in international law. However, she accepted the post, and quickly became known for her hard work, compassion, and dedication. In 1947, she was selected as the chairperson of the UN's Commission on Human Rights. Eleanor considered her service on this commission—specifically overseeing the drafting of the 1948 Universal Declaration of Human Rights—as her most important life's work. Crafting the document took many fourteen- and sixteen-hour work days, prompting one exhausted committee member to ask if Eleanor would also please consider her fellow delegates' human rights.

However, she accepted the post, and quickly became known for her hard work, compassion, and dedication.

Throughout her years at the UN, Eleanor traveled extensively around the globe observing political and socio-economic conditions in Europe, the Middle East, Asia, and the Pacific, and writing detailed accounts about all that she had seen in "My Day." At the end of 1952, Eleanor was asked to resign from her UN position by the newly elected—and very Republican—

Eleanor's appointment to the United Nations was viewed with skepticism by some, but those who served with her admired her tireless dedication to the rights of mankind.

Eisenhower administration. No doubt her active campaigning for Eisenhower's Democratic opponent had counted against her.

Eleanor's service at the UN had not been her only area of focus. She continued to strongly support causes in which she had long believed. Her activism on the part of civil rights, for example, had greatly strengthened since she had left the White House. In 1945, she had joined the board of directors of the NAACP and later served as vice president of that organization's Legal Defense and Education Fund. She also lent her support to other civil rights groups. FBI

The Universal Declaration of Human Rights

Within the newly established United Nations, a permanent Commission on Human Rights was formed to address educational and cultural issues, as well as policies for human rights standards. Among the members assigned to serve on the commission was Eleanor Roosevelt. In her memoirs, Eleanor mused that she was probably asked to serve there because it was thought to be a fairly "safe" (noncontroversial) committee in which her lack of experience might cause little harm. However, because of the many abuses that had occurred during World War II, human rights became a major issue for the UN almost immediately, and many were surprised by the intense dedication the former first lady brought to her new role.

One of the tasks the commission elected to take on almost immediately was to formulate a Universal Declaration of Human Rights that would clearly state the primary social, cultural, economic, political, and civil rights of mankind. A **subcommittee** was formed to draft the declaration, and Eleanor Roosevelt was asked to chair it. Over a period of two years, she firmly guided fellow delegates as they crafted this vital document. Presented to the UN General Assembly for adoption on December 10, 1948, this historic declaration still stands today—more than a half century later—its thirty articles spelling out in detail, and in more than 300 native tongues, those rights to which every person on Earth is entitled.

controversial activities and maintained a file on her for years. Now open to the public, Eleanor's FBI file is one of the largest on record. Nearly 90 percent of it pertains to her work for civil rights.

During the last decade of her life, Eleanor continued her travels around the globe. It was no wonder Harry Truman had called her the "First Lady of the World." She wrote two more volumes of her memoirs, contributed numerous articles to various publications, gave lectures to different groups, hosted a weekly interview program on television, spoke on the radio, and taught seminars on foreign policy at Brandeis University. Eleanor lived simply—either at her home at Val-Kill or the small apartment she rented in New York City. Children, grandchildren, and great-grandchildren came and went, along with famous and not-so-famous people. All were

A 1959 visit to Israel was one of three trips she made there. "Its young people," she wrote, "are excited by the dream of building a country and they work at it with gusto."

Attending a civil rights rally at New York's Madison Square Garden, Eleanor sits with Autherine Lucy, the first African American student to enroll at the University of Alabama.

welcome. "The greatest thing I have learned," Eleanor told a friend, "is how good it is to come home again."

In 1957, she traveled to the Soviet Union to interview the premier, Nikita Khrushchev, for the *New York Post.* She also campaigned actively for Democratic Party candidates, including Adlai Stevenson, and later, John F. Kennedy. In 1959, her son James wrote that "it is not an easy thing today to catch my fabulous mother in a state of repose, for Eleanor Roosevelt in her seventies is as active as I can remember in her fifties, if not more so."

In 1961, President Kennedy reappointed Eleanor as a delegate to the United Nations. He also asked her to serve on the

Advisory Council for the Peace Corps and later to chair the first President's Commission on the Status of Women. This twenty-member committee, made up of individuals who were active in women's rights, investigated questions regarding equality for women in the areas of legislation, education, and the workplace.

Final Years

As Eleanor Roosevelt neared eighty, she finally began to slow down, publishing only three "My Day" columns each week and lessening her extensive travels. Although her health began to seriously fail by the summer of 1962, she could not resist a last visit to Campobello—where a bridge extending between Canada and Maine was being dedicated in memory of her late husband.

By that fall, Eleanor was in and out of the hospital, and on November 7, 1962, not long after her seventy-eighth birthday,

Paying their respects at the funeral of Eleanor Roosevelt are President John F. Kennedy (left), former President Harry S Truman (center front), future President Lyndon B. Johnson (center back), and former President Dwight D. Eisenhower.

she died. Following her wishes, her simple oak coffin was covered with evergreen boughs from the Val-Kill woods, and she was buried beside her husband in the Hyde Park rose garden. In attendance were her five children, scores of family and friends, dignitaries from around the world, two former presidents (Harry S Truman and Dwight D. Eisenhower), the current president (John F. Kennedy), and a future president (Lyndon B. Johnson).

David Roosevelt later noted that his grandmother's funeral accomplished a nearly impossible feat: the uniting of many of the world's most powerful statesmen—both allies and **adversaries**—for a brief period of peace and accord. At a United Nations tribute to Eleanor Roosevelt, U.S. delegate Adlai Stevenson said, "I have lost more than a beloved friend. I have lost an inspiration. She would rather light a candle than curse the darkness, and her glow has warmed the world."

Wife, mother, first lady, diplomat, teacher, activist, author, visionary, humanitarian—no single description can sum up the unique spirit that was Eleanor Roosevelt.

119

GLOSSARY

activist—one who takes direct action to achieve a social or political goal.

adversaries—those who oppose or resist others; enemies.

alliance—a bond or tie between persons or groups that is based on common interests or goals.

apprentice—one who is learning a trade, art, or business.

Cold War—the nonviolent struggle for power that took place between the United States and the Soviet Union in the decades following World War II.

convention—a meeting of persons to select candidates for office.

delegation—one or more individuals appointed or elected to represent others.

extremist—one who believes or supports extreme or drastic views or ideas.

feminist—one who supports women's rights and interests and believes in the economic, political, and social equality of the sexes.

Great Depression—the decade-long period of worldwide economic crisis and massive unemployment that began in 1929.

gubernatorial—of or relating to the office of governor.

humanitarian—an individual who promotes or works for the health and welfare of others.

immigrant—a person who comes to a country to live there permanently.

landslide—an overwhelming political victory.

League of Nations—a political organization formed to promote world peace.

literacy—the ability to read and write.

racial discrimination—unfair or abusive behavior toward members of another race.

refugee—a person who flees to a foreign country for safety.

rehabilitation—the providing of help and treatment for physical disabilities through therapy and education.

segregation—the isolation or separation of a group, class, or race, especially as a form of discrimination.

settlement houses—social and cultural centers established in U.S. cities in the early twentieth century to help improve living conditions of poor people.

spokesperson—one who speaks for a group or another individual.

subcommittee—a portion of a committee organized for a specific purpose.

United Nations (UN)—international organization founded in 1945 to promote worldwide peace and economic development.

BIBLIOGRAPHY

Burns, James MacGregor and Susan Dunn. *The Three Roosevelts*. New York: Atlantic Monthly Press, 2001.

Caroli, Betty Boyd. *The Roosevelt Women*. New York: Basic Books, 1998.

Cook, Blanche Wiesen. *Eleanor Roosevelt: Volume One—1883–1933*. New York: Viking, 1992.

_____. *Eleanor Roosevelt: Volume Two—1933–1938*. New York: Viking, 1999.

Freeman, Russell. *Eleanor Roosevelt: A Life of Discovery*. New York: Clarion Books, 1993.

_____. *Franklin Delano Roosevelt*. New York: Clarion Books, 1990.

Goodwin, Doris Kearns. *No Ordinary Time: Franklin and Eleanor Roosevelt—The Homefront in World War II*. New York: Simon & Schuster, 1994.

Lash, Joseph. *Eleanor and Franklin*. New York: W. W. Norton, 1971.

_____. *Eleanor: The Years Alone*. New York: W. W. Norton, 1972.

Pottker, Jan. *Sara and Eleanor*. New York: St. Martin's Press, 2004.

Roosevelt, David B. *Grandmére: A Personal History of Eleanor Roosevelt*. New York: Warner Books, 2002.

Roosevelt, Eleanor. *The Autobiography of Eleanor Roosevelt*. New York: Harper & Row, 1978.

_____. *Tomorrow Is Now*. New York: HarperCollins, 1966.

Roosevelt, Elliott and James Brough. *An Untold Story: The Roosevelts of Hyde Park*. New York: G. P. Putnam Sons, 1973.

_____. *Mother R: Eleanor Roosevelt's Untold Story*. New York: G. P. Putnam's Sons, 1977.

Roosevelt, James. *My Parents: A Differing View*. Chicago: Playboy Press, 1976.

Roosevelt, James and Sidney Shalett. *Affectionately, F.D.R.* New York: Harcourt, Brace & Company, 1959.

Ward, Geoffrey. *Before the Trumpet: Young Franklin Roosevelt, 1882–1905*. New York: Harper & Row, 1985.

IMAGE CREDITS

ABOUT THE AUTHOR

Author Victoria Garrett Jones says, "Thirty years ago I was a student at
Vassar College, pursuing a degree in history. Once a week during my junior
year, I drove north a few miles along the Hudson River to Hyde Park and
volunteered at the Roosevelt home. As a docent, I was permitted to lift the
velvet ropes and step behind the scenes—to go where the average visitor
could not. During those hours each week, history truly came alive for me.
There was a reverence here, a sense of a hallowed place, a sense of lives
altered and dreams shifted. By the fireplace were two distinctive leather
chairs—one for Franklin and one for Sara but none for Eleanor. Upstairs
was Sara's large and beautifully furnished bedroom where her son had been
born. Nearby was Franklin's—spacious and sun-filled—with the famous
blue cape and the simple wooden wheelchair. But for Eleanor there was only
a small, narrow space wedged between Sara's and Franklin's. The room was
like a monk's cell in its simplicity. I found myself intrigued by this woman—
so famous, so admired, so accomplished, yet treated almost as an
afterthought in this house. Thus began my fascination with Eleanor
Roosevelt."

Jones is a freelance writer and former *National Geographic* researcher;
she lives with her husband and two children on Maryland's Eastern Shore.
This is her fifth publication for Sterling.

INDEX

Activism, of Eleanor, 3, 83–84, 86–95. *See also* Volunteer work
  civil rights, 87–90, 114–116
  DAR resignation, 90, 91
  death threat and, 87
  privileged life and, 50
  women's roles, 90–95
Activist, defined, 120
Adversaries, 119, 120
Air travel, 75, 99
Allenswood Academy, iv, 15–17, 22, 85
Anderson, Marion, 89, 90
Apprentice, 34, 120
Bethune, Mary, 88–89
Betrayal, by FDR, 44–45, 46, 104–106
Birth, of Eleanor, iv, 7
Campobello Island, 23, 36, 37, 41, 51, 58, 118
Child labor reform, 20–22
Children. See Family life
Churchill, Winston, 63, 101, 103, 104
Civilian Conservation Corps (CCC), 91–92
Civil Rights activism, 87–90, 114–116
Cold War, 1, 120
College Settlement volunteering, 24–25
Columnist. See "My Day" column
Convention, defined, 120
Criticism, taking, 94–95
Daughters of the American Revolution (DAR), 90, 91
Death, of Eleanor, iv, 118–119
Delegation to UN, 1–2, 113–114, 117
Earhart, Amelia, 75
Early years, iv, 12–19
  after mother's death, 12–15
  at Allenswood Academy, iv, 15–17, 22, 85
  birth, 7
  death of brother, 14–15
  death of father, 15
  death of mother, 10–11
  helping raise brother, 18–19
  relationship with father/mother, 7–9
  returning from Europe, 18–19

  separated from father, 9, 13
  unhappy childhood, 7, 12–15
Extremist group, 87, 120
Family life. *See also* Early years
  athletic/outdoor activities, 85
  balancing volunteering with, 42–43
  busy lifestyle straining, 62–65, 67–68
  children, 35, 36–37, 41, 42
  lack of closeness, 64–65
  last decade of life, 116–117
  missing FDR, 110
  political life and, 38, 39–41
  sons in World War II, 81
  in White House, 77
FBI files, on Eleanor, 116
Feminist, 16, 120
Final years, 118–119
Financial security, 34–35
First lady. *See also* Activism, of Eleanor
  addressing political convention, 96, 99
  firsts, 99
  flying in airplanes, 75
  leaving White House, 108–109
  press conferences by, iv, 73–74, 90, 99
  refusing benefits, 111
  reluctantly becoming, 70–72, 73
  social duties, 77
  of the world, 110–118
  World War II and, 81–84
Glossary, 120
Great Depression, 66, 67, 69, 72, 120
Gubernatorial election, 65, 120
Halsey, Admiral William, 82, 84
Hickock, Lorena "Hick," 71–72, 73, 76, 77
Howe, Louis, 39, 40, 45, 49, 52–53, 57, 65, 83
Humanitarian, 3, 120. *See also* Activism, of Eleanor; United Nations; Volunteer work
Immigrant population, 20, 34, 120
Junior League, 20
Kennedy, President John F., 63, 117–118, 119

Landslide, 65, 72, 120
League of Nations, 47, 120
League of Women Voters, iv, 50, 51, 73
LeHand, Missy, 77, 83
Literacy, 77, 120
Marriage, to FDR, iv, 2, 26–27
  betrayal, 44–45, 46, 104–106
  changed relationship, 46–47
  courtship before, 23–27
  honeymoon, 31
  meeting Franklin, 22–23
  wedding day, 30–31
Mercer, Lucy, 39–41, 42, 44–45, 46, 59, 104–106
"My Day" column, iv, 76–77, 78, 90, 111, 113, 118
New Deal, 67, 77–78, 87
Outdoor life, 85
Paralysis, of FDR, iv, 51, 52–53, 54–57, 59–60, 85
Parents. *See* Roosevelt, Anna Hall (mother); Roosevelt, Elliott (father)
Perkins, Frances, 91, 92
Politics. *See also* First lady; Roosevelt, Franklin Delano (FDR)
  FDR campaigns, 49, 65, 70–71
  move to Albany and, 37–38, 66
  move to Washington and, 39–41
  not running for office, 111–112
President's Commission on the Status of Women, iv, 118
Press conferences, iv, 73–74, 90, 99
Public life. *See also* "My Day" column; Activism, of Eleanor; First lady; Volunteer work
  rise of popularity and, 62–68, 80
  straining relationship with children, 62–65, 67–68
Racial activism, of Eleanor, 87–90
Racial discrimination, 87, 120. *See also* Civil Rights activism
Radio commentator, 62, 99, 116
Red Cross, iv, 42, 43, 82

Refugees, 81, 120
Rehabilitation, 52, 54, 120
Roosevelt, Anna Hall (mother)
  Eleanor relationship with,
    7, 9
  family background, 6
  illness/death of, iv, 10–11
  marriage to Elliott, 6
Roosevelt, Elliott (father)
  background, 4–5
  death of, iv, 15
  depression of, 4, 8, 11
  drinking problem, 5, 6, 7,
    8–9, 13
  Eleanor relationship with,
    7–9
  marriage to Anna, 6
Roosevelt family, 4–11. See also
  Family life; specific family
  names
Roosevelt, Franklin Delano
  (FDR). See also Marriage,
  to FDR
  as assistant secretary of
    navy, 39, 41, 43, 47
  background/, 23
  betraying Eleanor, 44–45,
    46, 104–106
  childhood, 23, 24
  courtship and love, 23–27
  cousin to Eleanor, 19, 23, 26
  death of, iv, 102–103
  decline in, 96–100
  funeral/train procession,
    106–108
  as governor, iv, 65–66, 69
  losses in 1941, 83
  meeting Eleanor, 22–23
  New Deal of, 67, 77–78, 87
  at 1924 Democratic
    Convention, 57
  with pneumonia/influenza,
    43–44
  polio/paralysis of, iv, 51,
    52–53, 54–57, 59–60
  as president, iv, 72, 77–78,
    96–100, 101–102
  as presidential candidate,
    70–72
  in state senate, iv, 37–38
  as vice-presidential
    candidate, 48–49
Roosevelt, Hall, 11, 12, 15,
  18–19, 83

Roosevelt, Sara
  death of, 83
  Eleanor/FDR marriage and,
    27, 31
  FDR affair and, 45
  FDR paralysis and, 52
  as FDR's mother, 23, 24
  homes given by, 35, 36, 58
  influence on Eleanor, 2–3,
    31, 35–36
  relationship with Eleanor,
    30–31, 35–36, 52, 64, 83
  space from, 38
Roosevelt, Theodore, Jr.
  (Uncle Ted)
  death of, 28, 47
  Eleanor and, 13
  Eleanor/FDR marriage
    and, 24, 27, 30, 32
  Eleanor's father and, 4, 9, 10
  family background, 4, 5
  life overview, 28–29
  political life, 18, 39
  wife and children, 12
Roosevelt, Theodore, Sr., 4, 5
Segregation, 88, 120. See also
  Civil Rights activism
Settlement houses, 84, 120
Social involvement. See
  Activism, of Eleanor;
  Volunteer work
Society life
  debut, iv, 19
  mixed feelings toward, 50–51
  Washington, D.C., 39–41, 77
Souvestre, Marie, 15, 16, 17,
  22, 31
Spokesperson, 95, 120
St. Elizabeth's Hospital, iv, 48
Stevenson, Adlai, 117, 119
Subcommittee, 115, 120
Thompson, Malvina "Tommy,"
  62, 76, 77
Timeline, iv
Tomorrow is Now, iv, 3
Travels
  last decade of life, 116–117
  throughout country, 66, 79
    for UN, 113
  updating FDR on, 80–81
  without special treatment,
    66–67, 79
  during World War II,
    81–82, 84

Truman, Harry S., 98,
  102–103, 104, 108, 112,
  113, 116, 118, 119
United Nations (UN), 101,
  112, 120
  delegate to, iv, 1–2, 3,
    113–114, 117
  established, iv, 113
  honoring Eleanor, 1
  name origin, 113
  Universal Declaration of
    Human Rights, iv, 1–2,
    113, 115
Universal Declaration of
  Human Rights, iv, 1–2,
  113, 115
Val-Kill, 61–62, 63, 110, 116
Van Rosenvelt, Claes
  Martenszen, 4, 5
Volunteer work
  child labor reform, 20–22
  College Settlement, 24–25
  Junior League work, 20
  League of Women Voters,
    iv, 50, 51, 73
  Navy League, 42–43, 48
  Red Cross, iv, 42, 43, 82
  Women's Trade Union
    League, iv, 53–54, 73
  World War I and, 43, 47–48
Warm Springs, 58–59, 102
Women
  in the CCC, 91–92
  in government, 90–91
  League of Women Voters,
    iv, 50, 51, 73
  right to vote, 49, 50
  roles of, Eleanor influencing,
    90–95
  World War II and, 92–95
Women's City Club of New
  York, 62
Women's Trade Union League,
  iv, 53–54, 73
Yalta Conference, 101–102, 103